PENGUIN VEER
BEYOND FEAR

Major General Ian Cardozo was commissioned at the Indian Military Academy into the 1st Battalion of the 5th Gorkha Rifles (Frontier Force), where he received his basic grounding as a young officer. Thereafter, he took part in the Sino–Indian war of 1962, the Indo–Pak war of 1965 and the Indo–Pak war of 1971.

Wounded in the battle of Sylhet in Bangladesh, he overcame the disability of losing a leg and became the first disabled officer of the Indian Army to be approved for command of an infantry battalion and brigade. He thereafter commanded an infantry division and retired as Chief of Staff of a corps in the North-east. On retirement, he worked in the area of disability with an NGO and as vice president of the War Wounded Foundation, before being appointed by the Government of India as chairman of the Rehabilitation Council of India, where he worked for nine years.

He is a military historian, author and war poet. His books, poems and autobiography, *Cartoos Saab*, have been widely acclaimed. His poems on war have been set to music and feature worldwide on leading music platforms. He is also working with an illustrator on graphic novels about the courage and competence of the Indian soldier, of which thirteen have been published so far.

Celebrating 35 Years of
Penguin Random House India

ADVANCE PRAISE FOR THE BOOK

'For years I have felt that the literature on the lives of armed forces personnel and how they have gradually acclimatized to changes in societal norms was inadequate. After the first glance at *Beyond Fear*, I see that gap has been filled by living legend Major General Ian Cardozo. His fearless expression throughout the book is remarkable. The most striking feature of his writing is that he has narrated incidents that have firmed his views on the ethos that the armed forces live by. There is continuity in the sequencing of events as they occurred, making for ease of reading and also generating a desire in the reader to ask, "What next?" A must-read and must-possess book for serving officers and veterans; more importantly, for students in the formative years of their careers. It will lay a strong foundation for professional soldiers and firm their view that "Nation First and Always" is the primary ethos'—Vice Admiral Shekhar Sinha, PVSM, AVSM, Nao Sena Medal and Bar (Gallantry) (retd)

'Enjoyed reading the details of these events in such easy-flowing stories. Thank you for sharing these with the world'—Lieutenant General Arun K. Sahni, PVSM, UYSM, SM, VSM, and former General Officer Commanding-in-Chief, Indian Army

'*Beyond Fear*, a collection of unique true stories from Ian Cardozo, is a delight to read! They bring before us, in unexpected ways, dimensions of human courage from actual situations in the lives of individual soldiers and their families. The author's skill as a consummate narrator, his deeply humanistic vision and his erudition as one of India's foremost military historians give depth to this book. Several of the stories serve to position acts of individual courage in the context of military campaigns fought by units of the Indian Army from the nineteenth century, through the two world wars, to present-day counter-insurgency operations. In the process, the book accentuates the role of tradition in ensuring the professional effectiveness of India's armed forces, be it in upholding the honour of a regiment's "colours", in ensuring soldiering as a generational commitment to the military profession or in keeping one's word. The stories illustrate how courage goes beyond fear to enable India's warriors to overcome the limitations of technology, to balance environmental protection with military discipline, to respond to emerging challenges in gender equality for combatants as well as the serving war-wounded. *Beyond Fear* fleshes out how the men and women of India's armed forces invariably put "country first", often making the supreme sacrifice, giving a poignant resonance to the inscription from the Kohima War Memorial: "For your tomorrow, we gave our today"'—Ambassador Asoke Mukerji, former Permanent Representative of India to the United Nations

'*Beyond Fear* is a great book about courage. These thirteen stories are tales of rare courage in defending the country; courage which is rare and rarefied. General Cardozo is a great storyteller and each story grips you with the action, surroundings and emotion. Enjoy this rare read!'—Shiv Shivakumar, operating partner, Advent International

'General Cardozo has mastered the art of storytelling. *Beyond Fear* is not simply a collection of anecdotes. It is a compilation of tales that showcases the gallantry and resilience of Indian soldiers. The stories are a medley of courage, faith and honour. They captivate the heart and evoke a sense of pride'—Tanushree Podder, author of *Boots, Belts, Berets*; *On the Double* and *Girls in Green*

'This book should be in the inspirational reading and not the military section of a bookshop. Every story makes you laugh or choke with emotion or sends a shiver of wonder down your spine—or sometimes all three. Major General Cardozo has done it again. As in his *1971: Stories of Grit and Glory from the Indo–Pak War*, he has narrated how honour, courage and love mould the armed forces. Yes, love. As he says, one doesn't normally associate the forces with love, but they do love. They love their country, its people, their fellow soldiers and their regiment or squadron or ship. This time he has done it through stories that are a kaleidoscope of situations, centuries, valour, grit and honour. It's difficult to choose a favourite story, but I clearly have one—about the Gorkha widow sending her sole surviving son to serve in the regiment to maintain her family ties with it. I have heard it many times from Sir and it always makes me cry. I can but only quote the general, "While the man in the street holds the armed forces in high esteem, he knows very little about them. These stories, it is hoped, will bring them closer to the men and women in uniform and inspire them to uphold these ideals." For military buffs, this covers Rajputs, Sikhs, Gorkhas and many other regiments, the air force, campaigns in the nineteenth century, World War I and II, post-Independence wars, insurgencies and Sri Lanka—though perhaps the settings can be anywhere. I must add that the general is ably aided by the striking sketches by Rishi Kumar and the general's son Dr Arun Cardozo. There is a distinct difference in styles between the two (and I got only one wrong in guessing them apart!). My last word: Thank you, Sir, for continuing to serve in this worthy way'—Gautam Hazarika, banker turned military history researcher

'Impeccable stories that touch the heart and make you want to narrate them to others. These narratives are unique in the sense that they are wrapped in plots of the armed forces and carry a suite of emotions—love and animosity, humour and rumour, beliefs and myths, joy and pain. This book will be equally loved by parents while they become storytellers to kids and to corporate leaders who can inspire their teams with these powerful lessons of true professionals'—Mohit Gupta, founder, FROB (Friends of Books)

BEYOND FEAR

True Stories on Life in the Indian Armed Forces

IAN CARDOZO

Bestselling author of
1971: Stories of Grit and Glory from the Indo–Pak War

PENGUIN
VEER

An imprint of Penguin Random House

PENGUIN VEER

USA | Canada | UK | Ireland | Australia
New Zealand | India | South Africa | China | Singapore

Penguin Veer is part of the Penguin Random House group of companies
whose addresses can be found at global.penguinrandomhouse.com

Published by Penguin Random House India Pvt. Ltd
4th Floor, Capital Tower 1, MG Road,
Gurugram 122 002, Haryana, India

First published in Penguin Veer by Penguin Random House India 2023

Sketches courtesy of Rishi Kumar, except on pages 46, 134, 160
and 198—sketches courtesy of Dr Arun Cardozo

ISBN 9780143460367

Typeset in Requiem Text by MAP Systems, Bengaluru, India
Printed at Thomson Press India Ltd, New Delhi

www.penguin.co.in

The year 2022 commemorated seventy-five years of India's independence from British rule. It also commemorated seventy-five years of the Indo—Pak war of 1947—48 and sixty years since the Sino—Indian war of 1962.

This book is dedicated to all those who 'put courage beyond fear and duty above death' during those difficult times, to ensure that India's sovereignty remained safe and secure.

Contents

Acknowledgements

I take this opportunity to thank my family and friends who encouraged me to put these stories into print, as well as individuals and institutions who have in some way contributed to these narratives.

I am grateful to all, and their names, in no particular sequence, are given below.

Meghna Girish
Brigadier V.H.M. Prasad
Anoushka Jain
Squadron Leader Rana T.S. Chhina, MBE
General Shankar Roy Choudhury, PVSM
Nilanjana Bardan
Colonel Jagjit Singh
Aparna Narayan Menon
Major Leena Dadhwal, SM
Priscilla Cardozo
Naik Jai Singh
Captain V.K. Sundaram, MC

Major General H.L. Davies, CB, CBE, DSO, MC
Nalini Samuel
Lieutenant General (Dr) V.J. Sundaram, PVSM, AVSM, VSM
Colonel Madan Bhatia
Lieutenant General Vijay Oberoi, PVSM, AVSM, VSM
Colonel D.P.K. Pillai, SC
Rifleman Neerbahadur Thapa
Major S. Kanian
Clari Cardozo
Major J. Sharma, SM
Shilpa Vijayan Cardozo
Group Captain O.P. Taneja, VrC
Major R.S. Arora, VrC
Colonel Charlie James
Vikram Cardozo
Colonel Hari Babu Vadde, VSM
Major General E.J. Kochekkan, AVSM, SM, VSM
Anita Cardozo
Monika Deshpande
Chandrakala Thapa
Rishi Kumar
Dr Arun Cardozo
Syamala G.
Colonel Clifton Marquis
Air Marshal Philip Rajkumar, PVSM, AVSM, VM
Brigadier (Bertie) Joginder Sinh, VSM
Rev. Fr Malachy O'Dwyer
Sandy Marquis
Havildar Narbahadur Thapa
1/5 Gorkha Rifles (FF)

2/5 Gorkha Rifles (FF)
3/5 Gorkha Rifles (FF)
4/5 Gorkha Rifles (FF)
17 Sikh (Tiger Paltan)
16 Light Cavalry
The Garhwal Rifles Regimental Centre
Centre for Armed Forces Historical Research
United Service Institution

In addition to the names of the individuals and institutions given above, I would also like to specially thank those who have played a major role in their contribution through their oral or written descriptions of events that have shaped the stories given below:

'Captain Courageous' is a story about how Captain Leena, a determined young woman doctor of the Army Medical Corps, fought the system to ensure that she could do her duty as a doctor of the armed forces in a combat scenario in Jammu and Kashmir, despite the military hierarchy's misgivings and how she made history in the process.

'Jai! Jai Singh!' is based on an episode narrated to me by Naik Jai Singh of the 16th Cavalry in 2010, while we were both waiting to have our artificial limbs repaired at the Artificial Limb Centre, Pune. The story brings home to the reader the futility of war, the effects of war on families and what they can do to achieve positive outcomes from the tragedies that war can cause.

'The Bent Bayonet' highlights the importance of discipline in conquering fear. The story narrates how soldiers of a battalion in a Sikh regiment implicitly follow the orders of their Commanding Officer to the detriment of their own safety. This story was narrated to me by Colonel Jagjit Singh who was commanding 17 Sikh at that time.

'It's Never Too Late' is a narration of the air raid on Pakistan's airfield at Sargodha in 1965, led by Wing Commander O.P. Taneja, VrC. I thank him for his input and clarifications on this story that has been written about by both Indian and Pakistani authors, who have been acknowledged within the story itself. The story shows the reader that it is never too late to recognize the courage displayed during war.

'Future Tense' is an interesting story about the ability of some people in India to decipher the past and foretell the future. Major Kanian is one of them. Anoushka Jain, a schoolgirl who read this story, gave me good inputs on how to improve the flow of this story.

'The Empty Chair' is a ghost story narrated to me by an officer of the Garhwal Rifles during a visit to Lansdowne. Whether or not one accepts the story to be true would depend on whether one believes in ghosts! The story is supported by an article written by a British officer of the Garhwal Rifles, Major General H.L. Davies, CB, CBE, DSO, MC, which provides input to parts of the episode. My granddaughter, Anita Cardozo, contributed substantially to the story's design.

'The Sign of the Cross' describes an incident in the life of an officer from a battalion of the Brigade of the Guards during a counter-insurgency operation somewhere in Manipur, in the North-east. The events that followed had important outcomes in the lives of the villagers who witnessed this skirmish. It also manifests the part that God can play in our lives.

'Matter of Honour' brings to centre stage the role of honour in the lives of soldiers of the Indian Army. This story highlights the importance of honour among the soldiers of a battalion of the Rajputs, which motivates them to place courage beyond fear and duty above death.

'Regimental Bonds' tells the story of a third-generation soldier killed in combat while serving with the 1st Battalion, the 5th Gorkha Rifles (FF). The story recounts how his mother copes with the situation in order to keep the link between family and battalion alive.

'Answer to a Prayer' is all about faith, or the lack thereof, in the Almighty and how God sometimes answers prayers in a strange way.

'Destiny' is a story narrated to me by my coursemate Lieutenant General V.J. Sundaram, PVSM, AVSM, VSM, about the life of his father, Captain V.K. Sundaram, MC, during World War II. The details have been corroborated by the regimental history of the 5th Gorkha Rifles (FF). The story is linked with the life of his father's friend, also a medical officer, which makes one wonder whether destiny is a matter of chance or choice.

'The Memento' is a story that reminds the reader that soldiers never receive monetary rewards for good work done in the execution of their duties, and when such rewards do come their way, they are unable to recognize this as compensation for work done well.

'Ward No. 21' is the story of a combination of incidents that took place in the upper officers' ward at the Command Hospital Pune. Lieutenant General Vijay Oberoi, PVSM,

AVSM, VSM, a battle casualty of the 1965 war, told me about what happened in the hospital after that war. These events, as well as my own experiences in the same ward following the 1971 Indo–Pak War, helped shape this story.

I would like to thank my friends Meghna Girish, Brigadier Madhav Prasad, Squadron Leader Rana Chhina, Nilanjana Bardan, Anoushka Jain, Aparna Menon and Nalini Samuel in particular for taking the time to read the stories and offer their comments and suggestions. Anoushka, a teenager, gave me useful insights into how young people could view these stories. Meghna Girish edited the stories several times before they were finally sent to the publisher.

I would also like to thank my daughters-in-law, Clari and Shilpa, for going through the stories and offering their feedback. It was in their homes in Bolton, the UK and Tokyo, Japan that I wrote most of these stories.

I also thank Rishi Kumar and Dr Arun Cardozo for the illustrations in this book.

Most importantly, I would like to thank my wife, Priscilla, for allowing me to spend time away from her in the autumn of our lives to write these stories.

Preface

'The greatest love a person can have for his friends is to give his life for them.'

John 15:13, New Testament

This book, *Beyond Fear*, is a collection of short stories that reflect life in the armed forces in war and peace. These stories are based on true incidents, supported by historical fact and embellished a little with my imagination. They reinforce the adage that 'real life is often stranger than fiction'.

These stories show the reader that fear is part of our everyday lives, that courage is the antithesis of fear and that we need to face our fears in order to get on with our lives and move forward.

Most of the characters in these stories are real, but wherever necessary, names and locations have been changed to protect privacy.

Notwithstanding the above, those whose stories are being told will, I am sure, recognize themselves and the part played by them in these real-life dramas. There are also many who have lived through these times and would recognize the incidents but may not know the whole story.

Men and women of the armed forces are brought up on the credo of: *Country first, and self last.* This is a way of life for us. Courage, honour, duty, discipline and sacrifice are values that are held in high esteem and are parameters by which persons in uniform judge themselves. Everyday battles become a testing ground for the conduct of service personnel, and it is the manner in which we live and behave in peace that determines how we will fight and do our duty in war.

I do hope these stories will give the civilian reader an insight into life in the armed forces—a profession that has no equal.

Ian Cardozo

Captain Courageous

Never underestimate the strength of a woman

The Colonel of the Regiment[1] of the 5th Gorkha Rifles (Frontier Force), a major general of the Indian Army, looked up at the young woman who had just been marched into the Commanding Officer's (CO) office. Dressed in her combat uniform, she stood at attention in front of him, looking serious and intense. She seemed little more than a girl, with her plait neatly tucked under her combat cap, boots highly polished and her combat uniform well-pressed. Her stance indicated that she was a fit young lady who knew what she wanted.

The Colonel of the Regiment turned his attention to the CO of the 3rd Battalion of this regiment—a tall, well-built officer reputed to be cheerful under any circumstance and to never lose his cool. He was standing quietly beside the Colonel of the Regiment.

'Why is she here, Charlie, and what's all this fuss about?'

The CO cleared his throat and said, 'Sir, the battalion is moving shortly to a combat zone in the Srinagar Valley. Captain Leena, our regimental medical officer, wishes to accompany the battalion. She has, however, been informed by higher headquarters that it will not be possible for her to move to the Valley due to considerations for her safety and that she will soon be posted to another unit in Jammu.

Captain Leena has still applied to move with the battalion within ten days. Her request has been turned down by the higher formation headquarters: brigade, division and corps.[2] So, as of now, she cannot come along with us.

'Captain Leena is unhappy with this decision, which she feels is highly discriminatory. I have personally spoken to the Brigade Commander and the staff officer handling this case at the division, but they are adamant that she cannot, in her own interest, move with us to the Valley.

'She now insists on seeing you formally in the hope that you, as Colonel of the Regiment, can turn things around.'

The general, in his capacity as Colonel of the Regiment, was on tour to meet the battalions of his regiment. It was expected of him to listen to the officers and men of the regiment and find solutions to problems outside of the formal, hierarchical system. He had been recently appointed as Colonel of the Regiment. This was the first issue he was facing, and it did not appear to be an easy one.

'She has a point, Charlie,' the general said. 'What are your recommendations on her accompanying the battalion to the Valley?'

'I would like her to come along, Sir.'

Colonel Charlie James was a man of few words. He was a second-generation officer of the regiment. His father had commanded this very battalion many years earlier. Charlie was kind but firm, and he took no nonsense from anyone. He was never intimidated by rank and believed in speaking his mind to a point, after which he carried out orders. He genuinely believed that Captain Leena ought to accompany his battalion to the Valley, as its RMO.[3]

After some reflection, the general asked, 'What is the case being made out by higher headquarters that is preventing Captain Leena from going to the Valley?'

'Their view, Sir, is that firstly, the living conditions in counter-terrorist operational areas in the Valley are extremely harsh. They feel that Captain Leena has no idea how difficult these conditions can be. Secondly, by sending her to a combat zone in the Valley, she would be exposed to unacceptable levels of danger. The battalion is bound to get involved in fights against terrorists and her life would be at risk. Any harm to her would be unacceptable to the hierarchy. Finally, if anything happens to her, there will be a lot of questions asked, and the media will have a field day criticizing the Army. We would get very bad press.'

'What else?'

'That's about it, Sir.'

The general sat silent for a moment.

'The issue, Charlie, as I see it, is that Captain Leena is a woman. The system needs to get used to the idea that women doctors can be as efficient as men in combat areas or anywhere else. Male medical officers have been courageous under fire and have proven this in two world wars and all the wars, counter-terrorist operations and counter-insurgency operations that our country has fought since Independence. The problem is that women medical officers have never been given the opportunity to prove themselves in similar combat situations.

'Statistics do not indicate that a large number of medical officers have become casualties in combat scenarios. Also, Captain Leena is a doctor in uniform and is, therefore, liable to risk and danger like all other Army doctors. Logically, she is right when she says that the Army is being discriminatory through excessive concern over her safety. She has personally volunteered to accompany the battalion to a combat zone. She, more than anyone else, understands her duties, responsibilities and accountability as a doctor in uniform and the risks involved. We need to give her the opportunity and space to prove herself. Finally, I don't see why anyone should come in the way of this young woman, who is only trying to do her duty. She is not performing a combat role; she is only doing her duty as a doctor.'

The general turned his attention to Captain Leena, who was still standing at attention and listening attentively to the proceedings.

'At ease, Captain Leena, at ease,' the general said and went on to ask, 'So, what do you have to say, Captain Leena? Are you confident of being able to function effectively in a combat scenario?'

'Yes, Sir!' Captain Leena said emphatically, springing to attention once again.

'Anything else, Captain Leena?' the general asked.

'No, Sir,' the regimental medical officer replied.

'All right, then. You may leave,' the general said. 'You can plan on accompanying the battalion.'

Captain Leena hesitated. She wondered whether he understood the implications of the problem and the full measure of the opposition he would have to face before such a decision could be taken. The general seemed to sense her quandary. He smiled and repeated, 'You may leave, Captain Leena.'

Captain Leena saluted smartly and marched off.

The general now turned to the CO and said, 'To continue, Charlie, you must be aware that women in uniform all over the world are clamouring for entry into the combat arms. Although the Indian Army has turned down this demand for very good reasons, I see this as an opportunity to meet that desire in a small way.[4] I know allowing Captain Leena to serve in a combat zone is not the same as allowing women into the combat arms, but at the same time, it is an opportunity to allow women medical officers to prove themselves in combat conditions. Women medical officers have served in war zones in the past, but mostly in hospitals, well behind the front line. We now have a unique situation on our hands, when, for the first time, we have a lady doctor volunteering to serve as an RMO in a front-line combat environment. We need to give her the opportunity to prove herself. Who knows? Maybe we are in the process of witnessing her make history.'

The general continued, 'We do not have much time, Charlie, so we need to act fast. Can you please get me the Brigade, Division and Corps Commanders on the line, one at a time and in that order?'

The calls were quickly put through and the telephone exchange buzzed with the activity generated by these calls. All three Commanders agreed to see the general, as he was known to them all. Fortunately, all three headquarters were not far from the battalion, and the three visits could be managed in a single day.

As appreciated by the general, the basic issue was: Who would be responsible for the decision, and who would be answerable if something went wrong? These would be the main points of discussion with all three Commanders.

The Colonel of the Regiment was aware of the risks involved. Although he accepted and appreciated Captain Leena's eagerness and passion to do her duty, he also knew she had not been through the tough training that officers of the Indian Army have to go through before and after being commissioned.

While driving to the Brigade Commander's office, he recalled his own days at the Indian Military Academy and his battalion, where the focus was to turn boys into men. He recalled the hard training they were put through to ensure they would not flinch in the heat and fire of battle. He remembered the tough forced marches over never-ending days and sleepless nights, often without food and water; the unambiguous code that no casualty was to be left behind; the battle inoculation under realistic warlike conditions that brought artillery, mortar and machine-gun fire so close that one could feel the heat of the rounds, smell the cordite and see the splintering effect of high explosive; the confidence that comes from unarmed combat and bayonet fighting and the use of the kukri and the sense of empowerment that comes from hard training. All this had not been part of Captain Leena's military background. However, he also knew intuitively and from his experience that she had the right character qualities, attitude and sense of purpose to see her through this assignment, however tough it turned out to be.

The general met the Brigade, Division and Corps Commanders in quick succession. All three stuck to their decision that Captain Leena should not go to the Valley, basically for reasons of her personal security.

The Corps Commander, however, stated, 'It does not matter to me whether the regimental medical officer is a man or a woman. What matters to me is that they have to be efficient in what they do. I agree with your view that she is only carrying out her role as a doctor, but the main issue is: What would happen if she got killed or wounded? In any case, I have forwarded my views to the medical directorate at Army Headquarters. I do not have a problem if the medical directorate is agreeable with Captain Leena accompanying the unit to the Valley, but they will need to communicate their views to me soon.'

The Colonel of the Regiment returned to the battalion. The visits had taken up a major part of the day, and it was late evening by the time he returned to the battalion. The battle had not been won, but it had not been lost either. After all, the Corps Commander had said that the Colonel of the Regiment was free to tackle the medical directorate and that was exactly what he would do. It was where the solution appeared to lie. The Colonel of the Regiment also realized that this issue would take more time than anticipated and wondered whether he would have to alter his tour schedule.

When the Colonel of the Regiment returned to his room in the officers' mess, Naik Balbahadur Gurung, the orderly detailed to look after him, informed him that the evening meal was a formal 'dinner night' in the officers' mess. Balbahadur had checked with the mess secretary on the dress for dinner and had got the general's medals polished and the mess dress ready. The general already knew this would be a dinner night,[5] but he was impressed that the NCO had also checked.

Naik Balbahadur had been wounded during the Indo–Pak War of 1965. His left arm had been amputated due to gunshot wounds, but this in no way affected his performance as a soldier. He had learnt to use his artificial limb and was as good as any other soldier at shooting on the range, in unarmed combat and everything else. In fact, he was way ahead of the others in map-reading and education, and was due for promotion to havildar and command of a section.

The general realized that the CO had intentionally placed Balbahadur as his helper because, as Colonel of the Regiment, he had issued guidelines as to the manner in which war-disabled service personnel were to be rehabilitated in the regiment and that they needed to be given every opportunity to prove themselves in the performance of their duties. The general was himself war-disabled, having lost a leg in the Indo–Pak War of 1971. He had single-handedly fought the system and proven to the military establishment that efficient war-disabled soldiers remained as good, if not better, than the non-disabled. He was, in fact, the pioneer in opening up promotion for war-disabled officers and men in the Indian Army.

The general took a bath, got dressed and went to the officers' mess, where he found the officers of the battalion waiting for him. Captain Leena was present too, but her mess dress was from the Army Medical Corps. The differences were in the cummerbund—the broad band of silk that officers wore around their waists—and her metal badges of rank, which were not black like those of a rifle regiment. There were also differences in the miniature badges that she wore on her collar, known as 'collar dogs'.

The Colonel of the Regiment briefed the CO as to what had transpired between him and the Formation Commanders on the issue of Captain Leena's move to the Valley. He had just finished when a mess waiter came up with a sheet of paper on a silver salver. All conversation stopped. The battalion second-in-command picked up the sheet and said, 'Sir, it's a signal from Army Headquarters.' The CO requested permission from the Colonel of the Regiment for the message to be read out and, having received his assent, read out the message. The message said:

MS-37659 Capt C Sharma, medical officer 123 GH, posted as RMO 3/5 GR (.) Officer to report immediately without relief (.) MS-37319 Capt Leena posted as RMO 7/9 GR (.) Capt Leena to move on relief (.) ack (.) All info

The message was listened to in silence. The CO and Captain Leena looked at each other in dismay. The situation, which had just moved a couple of steps forward, was now back at square one!

The general was the first to speak. He said, 'There is no need for all of you to look so glum. Charlie, please get me this number at Delhi.' He took out a small notebook and read out a telephone number.

He said, 'Colonel Anurag Mathur is the officer-in-charge of postings in the medical directorate. He was my regimental medical officer many years ago when I was commanding the First Fifth. He will have to help. It should not be too difficult. After all, we are asking for a posting to an operational area and not a peace posting to Delhi, Madras, Bangalore or Bombay!'

'What about Captain Sharma?' asked the CO.

The general said, 'That should not be a problem. Captain Sharma can be posted to another field area, if that is the requirement.'

A bugle call interrupted their conversation.

Bells and bugle calls regulate life in the Army. There were bugle calls to wake you up and bugle calls to tell you that it was time to go to sleep. There were bugle calls for meals, parades, games, fire alarms, emergencies and for every conceivable activity. The bugle call that just played was a mess call signalling it was time for dinner. The mess havildar[6] came in to report that dinner was ready and that it was time to move to the dining room.

The table was set in accordance with the time-honoured custom of an old regiment. Each officer had a designated place according to his or her seniority, with place cards indicating the place of seating. Crockery, cutlery and glasses with the regimental crest were placed to conform to the menu of the evening, which was scripted on menu cards set in silver menu stands. Silver trophies were placed at intervals on the table; each piece represented a particular fragment of the battalion's history, of battles fought in different parts of the world many years ago, as well as in recent times. Each piece of silver was contributed by officers, individually or collectively. The silver gleamed in the reflection of the lights that lit up the table and gave the whole scene an old-world ambience. Outside, the pipes and drums played regimental tunes, which wafted into the dining room with the evening breeze. The officers did not know that it would be many years before the battalion would have a gathering like this again. They would soon be involved in the dust and grime of battle—a different world altogether!

Dinner was quiet; each one stayed with their own thoughts.

The general looked across the table at Captain Leena to reassess her in his own mind. He saw in her, once more, the determination of a young woman who was prepared to prove to the world that she was as good, if not better, than a male regimental medical officer.

Captain Leena was also engrossed in her own thoughts. She was peeved that the male establishment was not prepared to give her a chance to prove herself. In that respect, the arrival of the Colonel of the Regiment was a godsend. He and her CO were the only two exceptions who believed in her, and she told herself that she would go all out, if only she was given the chance, to prove that they were right.

The CO, too, had a lot on his mind. The command of a battalion in a counter-terrorist environment was the acid test of a unit's ability, and he had done all that was possible to forge his battalion into an efficient and effective fighting machine. That included the regimental medical officer and her medical platoon. Captain Leena had risen to the challenge and proved her worth in all the test exercises. Why then, he asked himself, were they unable to understand that she was an integral part of the team and that the battalion would be able to take care of her safety, if that was all that they were bothered about? They had just finished dessert when a waiter brought the telephone to the CO. 'Phone call from Delhi, Sir,' the waiter said in Nepali.

Dinner night is a parade, and telephone calls are not allowed to disturb the equanimity of a dinner night except for very special circumstances. The mess havildar, however, seemed to have understood the importance of the call and had sent a waiter in with the instrument.

The CO took the call and, after ascertaining that it was for the general, he said, 'It's for you, Sir. Will you take the call now, or shall I tell him we will call back later?'

'I'll take the call now,' the general said, picking up the phone. It was from Colonel Anurag Mathur of the medical directorate, Army Headquarters.

'Anurag,' the general said. 'Sorry to bother you. We have a problem, and we need your help.'

The general first complimented the medical directorate for being innovative in posting a lady medical officer to an all-male infantry battalion, but added that the medical directorate now needed to take this issue to its logical conclusion and let her accompany the battalion to an operational area. He then went on to say that a signal had just been received for the posting of Captain Leena to another unit in a peace station and that the battalion was very upset at this turn of events. He then recounted all that had happened since his arrival, including his dialogues with the Formation Commanders and the logical reasons as to why Captain Leena should go with the battalion.

Colonel Anurag listened quietly to what the general had to say and replied, 'I will do what I can, Sir. I am sure you are aware that cancelling a posting order is not easy. Moreover, Captain Sharma needs to go to an operational area. However, let me see what I can do. I will get back to you tomorrow.'

The general changed his plans for his departure and said he would wait for the call. The call came through sometime around noon the next day, when the general was in the CO's office. Colonel Anurag Mathur was on the line.

'The medical directorate is not happy, Sir,' he said. 'They have cited three reasons why this posting cannot be cancelled. First, Captain Leena's posting was done at the request of the corps headquarters, and the corps has, so far, not changed its recommendations.

'Second, the posting of the officer replacing her has already been issued. This officer has never been to an operational area, and there have already been calls from influential people to change his posting. The medical directorate does not want the posting changed, as it would send out the wrong message.

'Third, the medical directorate is ambivalent about sending a lady medical officer to a high-risk combat zone.'

'Hmmm,' the general said. 'Any suggestions?'

'Off the record, Sir?'

'Yes, of course, Anurag.'

'Well, Sir, I spoke to my director and mentioned the advantages that you had outlined, of allowing Captain Leena to accompany the battalion to an operational area, and he saw the merits of your argument. I emphasized the fact that it would bring credit to the Indian Army Medical Corps in particular, and to women and the Army in general.

'The decision taken, however, was that notwithstanding the fact that the roles of the formations are recommendatory in nature, they can only review the case if the Corps Commander changes his recommendations. As far as Captain Sharma is concerned, it would be possible to post him to another equally difficult operational area. This would help us do the right thing and would also meet everyone's requirements. Another factor that was a matter of concern to the medical directorate was: What would be the attitude and reaction of the media if something untoward were to happen to Captain Leena?'

'The media,' the general replied, 'would go by whatever makes news. If Captain Leena does well, she will make news; if something untoward happens, that will also make news. We should, however, not take counsel from our fears. Every aspect of this issue has been examined, and we are confident that all will go well. Yes, there is always the factor of the unknown, but that is a risk we need to take. Is the Army not known to be an institution that factors risk-taking as one of the important elements in decision-making? We know what we are doing, and we are aware of the risks involved. We, however, need to do what we think is right and then go ahead with full energy and resolve.'

'Yes, Sir,' Anurag said, listening carefully and absorbing the general's words.

'One more thing, Sir,' he added. 'It would also be necessary for Captain Leena to furnish a certificate saying that she would be solely responsible for her decision to serve in a high-risk combat zone.'

The last part of the dialogue was encouraging, as it appeared to suggest that the situation continued to be open-ended. 'That will not be a problem, Anurag.' The general thanked Colonel Anurag and put the phone down. It was now quite clear that the decision on this matter had shifted back to the Corps Commander.

Just at that moment, there was a call from the corps headquarters. The CO took the call.

It was the staff officer to the Corps Commander who said, 'Colonel Tejinder here, Sir. Good afternoon. The General Officer Commanding has asked me to ask you whether it would be all right for him to visit the battalion tomorrow at 1100 hours to meet all of you before you leave for the Valley. As you are aware, this visit was planned for the day after tomorrow, but the Corps Commander has been called to Delhi, hence the change of plans.'

The CO said that it would be all right and that the battalion would be awaiting the arrival of the Corps Commander at 1100 hours.

The CO turned to the general and said, 'Looks good, Sir; we have been given one more opportunity to help the Corps Commander change his mind.'

The Corps Commander arrived at the appointed time. All personnel of the battalion were assembled at the battalion durbar hall. They were all wearing their combat uniforms, sitting cross-legged on the ground in straight rows and columns, with the officers and junior commissioned officers (JCOs) on chairs on either side.

The CO reported to the Corps Commander that the battalion was assembled and ready for his address.

The Corps Commander put all those who had assembled at ease and spoke to the men about the tasks they were likely to face in the Valley and how they should respond. He explained to them that their job was not an easy one and they had to combine military professionalism with a balanced approach and kindness towards civilians in general and women, children and old people in particular.

He explained the difference between the rights and responsibilities of both civilians and military personnel in anti-terrorist operations. He explained that, as far as the terrorists were concerned, they were to be professional in eliminating them in combat and to follow the Geneva Conventions. He emphasized that despite the difficulties they would face, they should never, ever do anything that could bring dishonour to their battalion and to the Army.

He then wished them all the very best and said that he would be keeping track of their performance and that he would visit them in the Valley after they had settled down.

The Corps Commander's address was followed by tea with the men, the JCOs and the officers. After tea, the Corps Commander chatted with the men and then came around to the officers to talk with them before leaving.

It was during this time that he came face-to-face with Captain Leena.

On seeing her, he asked, 'So, are you the one who wants to go to the Valley on combat duty?'

Leena got the opening that she wanted. 'Yes, Sir,' she said and waited.

The Corps Commander paused too, and there was an awkward silence.

Leena then used the opportunity to speak. 'Sir, I am inspired by what you have just said, but I have been left out of it all, because you are not allowing me to go and perform my duty. I am an Army doctor, and being a woman should not bar me from my duty and doing all those things that you just talked about. On the one hand, you say that we should do our best for the country, and when we volunteer to do our bit, we are not allowed to do so. This is most unfair and discriminatory. In fact, I am being prevented from doing my duty by old-fashioned ideas and excessive concern by those who are not aware of the ability and potential of women doctors. My Commanding Officer wants me to go with the battalion, so why should anyone else object? I have given it in writing that I am aware of the dangers I could face and I am fully prepared to accept them. I have also mentioned that, if anything happens to me, no one else is responsible. Sir, please let me accompany my battalion.'

The Corps Commander was taken aback by Captain Leena's emotional outburst. She, in fact, was on the verge of tears. He probably did not expect the intensity of purpose and determination of this young lady, who refused to take the easy way out or 'no' for an answer.

There was pin-drop silence all around, and everyone was eager to hear what the Corps Commander would say.

The Corps Commander knew that he had to take a decision right there and then. A bureaucratic answer would not do. He was aware that the battalion wanted Captain Leena to go with them to the Valley. He understood better than anyone else the meaning of motivation and morale in the Army and the possible repercussions of his answer.

Turning to the CO, he said, 'Your Colonel of the Regiment has also discussed this matter with me. Having heard this young lady and taking into consideration your recommendation and that of your Colonel of the Regiment, I feel that perhaps I can review my decision. However, the Army Headquarters will have to be informed.

I will discuss this issue with them, but the staff work will have to be done by you. Send your proposal to the medical directorate, Army Headquarters, with a copy to me. Quote today's meeting and say that I have accepted Captain Leena's application to go along with the battalion. Your proposal should be sent by signal today itself, so that it reaches Army Headquarters well before I meet the staff of the medical directorate tomorrow.'

He turned back to Captain Leena. 'Well, then, you have got what you want. You can go with the battalion. Do well and best of luck.' He shook hands with her, the CO, the subedar major and the Colonel of the Regiment, then got into his car, which had been backed up to where they had gathered, and drove away.

Captain Leena was happy and excited. She could not conceal her joy. The Colonel of the Regiment, the CO and the other officers present were all smiling. Everyone in the battalion was delighted.

The Colonel of the Regiment realized that his job was done. He decided to leave the same evening to visit other units of his regiment after spending some time with Captain Leena. He sent for her, and she came smiling and happy that, at last, she had got what she wanted so desperately.

He said, 'Leena, all of us are glad that you will finally be going with the battalion to the Valley. You, however, need to know that it isn't going to be easy. Being in a combat environment is quite different from what you have been used to in a peacetime cantonment. You need to prepare yourself mentally for situations where you will be under fire and yet have to carry on with your job; the possibility of being on the march for days and nights without sleep; the lack of privacy as a woman; and situations where life and death are part of everyday life. I am not trying to frighten you, but you need to be prepared for all the physical, mental and psychological challenges that you may have to face.'

Leena thought to herself, 'He's talking to me just like my father.'

She said, 'Don't worry, Sir. I have been thinking about all this myself. I will be all right, and I won't let you down.'

The Colonel of the Regiment smiled, shook hands with her and wished her all the best before leaving.

The battalion, in the meantime, got the necessary clearance from the medical directorate, and her posting order to the other unit was cancelled. The unit continued to prepare for its role in the Valley. Half the battalion was on the range testing their weapons and rehearsing counter-terrorist drills, while the remainder was busy packing for the move. Captain Sanjay, the adjutant, was given the task of preparing Captain Leena for her role in the Valley.

The battalion moved soon after by road to their destination in the Valley. The journey was an eye-opener for Captain Leena. The road to Srinagar, with its spirals and hairpin bends, was an engineering miracle, and she marvelled at the skill of the Army engineers who had built it. The sun was out in all its glory and the weather was at its best. As she sat in an open jeep with the wind in her face, she felt exhilarated with the realization that she was actually moving with the battalion for combat operations, and when she looked back and down below, she could see the vehicles of the convoy snaking across the twists and turns of the road as far as her eye could see. She felt privileged to be part of this experience.

Higher up on the road to the Valley, pine trees gave way to stately firs. They were at a higher altitude now, but winter had not yet arrived to drape these huge Christmas trees with mantles of snow. The Srinagar Valley had trees not normally seen in the rest of India. They were the poplar, the birch, the beech, the oak and the majestic chinars. It was autumn, and the trees on the slopes of the hills were a blaze of yellow, orange, ochre and gold. The leaves of the huge chinar trees had turned blood-red, and she wondered apprehensively whether this colour was a harbinger of events that were yet to unfold!

She was, however, happy and excited that she had finally been given the opportunity to be with this battalion and to prove herself—not only for the women doctors in the Army but for all women in general. She also realized she would face tough times ahead, and she strengthened her resolve to live up to the expectations of the CO of the battalion, the Colonel of the Regiment and the Corps Commander.

On arrival in the Valley, the battalion learnt that they would be inducted into an area where terrorist activity was particularly high. Initially, they would be deployed with another brigade for 'on-the-job training'. The day after the battalion arrived, all officers were called for a briefing by the Brigade Commander who was to train them. It was mentioned during the briefing that a male RMO would be attached to the battalion for the duration of the training in actual operations.

The CO thought to himself, 'Here we go again. The same story, and the same attitudinal problems as to how you can have a lady RMO functioning in operations against terrorists.' He decided not to say anything just yet, as this embargo applied only to the period of training, which was only a matter of four weeks, and once they reverted to their own brigade, Captain Leena would be back in position.

After the briefing, the training Brigade Commander asked everyone concerned if they had any questions. To everyone's surprise, Captain Leena stood up and said, 'Sir, I have a question. May I know why you are removing me from my command?'

There was pin-drop silence, and all the officers present wondered what would happen next.

'What command?' the brigadier asked, looking irritated and a little perplexed.

'The command of my medical platoon, Sir,' she replied.

Everyone tried to keep a straight face, but some smiled. Captain Leena, however, was dead serious.

The Brigade Commander did not have an immediate answer, but he was not amused. Looking at Captain Leena, he said firmly, 'Sit down, young lady,' before turning to the CO. 'See me later. This nonsense must stop.'

Later, at tea, the CO explained the situation to the brigadier. But the brigadier was exasperated and not prepared to listen. He said, 'Look, this is not an area for women to be messing around with terrorists, okay? Your one month of training involves live operations, and as long as you are with me, I am sending you a male RMO and that's it.'

After one month, the battalion reverted to its parent brigade upon completion of its on-the-job training and settled down to its operational tasks. Captain Leena returned to the battalion.

Sometime later, Leena had her baptism by fire, and she did not come out with flying colours. The CO had to attend a conference at the brigade headquarters. Leena wanted to go along with him as she had to get some medicines from the field ambulance that was co-located with the brigade headquarters. They were on their way when they were ambushed by terrorists. Leena was in the co-driver's seat of the one-ton truck following the CO's jeep. The one-ton had a light machine gun mounted on the top of the driver's cabin, and it started firing in response to the high volume of fire from the terrorists. The Quick Response Team (QRT) accompanying the CO had already dismounted and was moving behind the terrorists to cut them off. The CO was busy responding to the situation on his radio set. He turned around and discovered that Leena was still glued to her seat in the one-ton vehicle.

He shouted, 'Leena, move! Get out quickly!' But she did not seem to hear him. The CO's runner realized Leena could get hit because the one-ton was drawing heavy fire from the terrorists. He dashed across, opened the door of the one-ton and pulled Leena out. No sooner had he done so than a burst of machine-gun fire from the terrorists smashed through the windscreen of the vehicle, exactly where she had been sitting. He was able to get her out just in the nick of time.

The ambush led to a cordon and search operation, and the battalion was able to kill two terrorists and capture a third. They also recovered a machine gun, three rifles, some explosives and a bag of grenades. When the operation was over, the CO sent for Leena.

He said, 'Leena, why did you not get out of the vehicle when all that firing was going on? Were you not briefed on the drills to be followed during an ambush?'

She said, 'I'm sorry, Sir. I just don't know what happened to me. This is the first time I've personally come under fire, and I just froze and could not move. This is the first and last time something like this will happen.'

True to her word, the next time Captain Leena came under fire, she responded like a seasoned soldier. A rifle company was out on an area dominance patrol. They were mounted on vehicles. The CO was required to attend a conference at the brigade headquarters and Leena asked him if she could go along to replenish her medical supplies. While the CO and Leena were on their way, the CO's radio operator, who was in contact with the area dominance patrol, told him that the patrol had been ambushed and suffered three casualties. The CO spoke to the Brigade Commander on the radio and briefed him about what had happened, and they changed direction and moved quickly to the ambush site. When they reached the site, they came under heavy fire. Leena, however, was out in a jiffy, and despite the bullets that were flying around, she went straight to the injured soldiers.

One boy had taken a bullet through his ankle; a second in his arm; and the third was lying on a stretcher soaked in blood from the waist down. He had taken

a machine-gun burst in his groin. There was a nursing
assistant on the patrol. He had dressed the arm and
ankle injuries, but was at a loss as to what to do with the
abdominal injury. Without batting an eye, Leena pulled
down the boy's pants and got to work to stem the blood
flow, all the while screaming at the nursing assistant
that this casualty should have been attended to first.
She managed to stop the blood flow with whatever was
available and asked for a helicopter evacuation, as the
boy had lost a lot of blood and would go into shock if
they were not able to get him to the hospital in time. The
chopper arrived within thirty minutes, and thanks to
Leena, the boy survived. She had displayed a great deal of
professionalism and courage under fire.

By this time, news had got around to the media that
a woman medical officer was operating in the Valley with
the Army in combat operations and that her life was in
grave danger. The media pounced on this revelation, and
headlines in the newspapers triggered responses from
women's groups. The Society for the Protection of Women
clamoured for her safety and asked that she be protected
from a 'cruel and heartless' Army that was using women
in such a dangerous role and that she be removed from the
front line immediately. Politicians got wind of it, and the
issue became politicized. They began to make inquiries,
asking if this were true, and internal discussions were
held to work out how this cause could best be utilized
for garnering women's votes for their respective parties.
Fortunately, another women's group, Action for the
Development and Ability of Women, sided with the Army,

stating that this was a step in the right direction for the emancipation of women. They also stated that the Army needed to make sure that all steps were taken to ensure adequate protection of the lady doctor.

The politicians were now in a quandary. The Ministry of Defence knew that if anything untoward happened to the lady doctor, there would be a lot of awkward questions, and they might not have the right answers. Pressure was now mounting on the Army to quietly get Captain Leena removed from the danger zone. The Ministry of Defence asked Army Headquarters to review the situation. They, in turn, asked the medical directorate for their response. Ultimately, the issue landed in the lap of the Corps Commander, who was asked to respond before the situation got out of hand. The question was, 'Who would blink first?'

The Corps Commander, however, was made of sterner stuff. He gave the following statement: 'I am perfectly aware of the risks involved and assure all concerned that the lady doctor is not involved in a combat role but only in a combat situation where she is well-protected. My decision will not change, and I take full responsibility for my decision.' The controversy did not die down, and news items and letters to the editor in various newspapers kept the issue alive.

Meanwhile, operations in the Valley continued. In another incident, Captain Leena once again displayed courage and commitment of a very high order in the line of fire. The battalion was going out on a cordon and search operation that was in an interior area and involved a full night's march. According to laid-down orders, the battalion QRT along with the medical team and ambulance were required to fetch up at first light only after the cordon had been put into place. The CO had repeatedly told Leena that it would be better if she came with the ambulance. She would, however, always insist on going with the battalion along with the medical team. After some time, the CO gave up, and she would accompany the battalion whenever they were out on operations, no matter what the duration was. At times, the battalion would be away for six to seven days as they would get information about a group of terrorists, and one operation would lead to another and then another. Never once did she say that she was tired or that she needed a break.

During this particular operation, while the battalion was skirting a village, the leading company was fired upon. It was around 9 p.m. and pitch dark. The companies deployed, and there was a heavy exchange of fire. One of the boys was hit in the abdomen by a machine-gun burst, and the CO asked for the RMO. Leena was part of the CO's party, which was right behind the leading company. They moved forward in the dark, guided by the Company Commander, until they reached the injured boy, who was lying in the open. Despite the fact that the area was the focus of much firing, Leena went to tend to him without hesitation. However, with bullets zipping all around, it became difficult to attend to him, so they had to drag him to the cover of a hut. Leena was totally unmindful of the bullets and shrapnel flying around during the entire time. Once they got the boy into the hut, she attended to him with a torch as no other light was available. The boy's name was Lalbahadur, and he was bleeding heavily.

Leena told the CO that Lalbahadur had to be evacuated to the hospital soon, as he had lost a lot of blood. The CO told her there was no chance of getting through to the ambulance, as all communication with the base had broken down, and she had to keep the casualty going till first light or until they were able to re-establish communication with the base or with the brigade. They then organized a stretcher, and the boys had to carry the casualty, which was a Herculean task as they were operating cross-country and in hilly terrain. Around 1 a.m., Leena once again told the CO that it was imperative to get the wounded boy to a hospital or they would lose him.

The CO decided to hold the battalion for a while and tried to get in touch with the base. They had to climb a hill in an attempt to re-establish contact, and they finally managed to get through. The CO ordered the QRT to move, although it was against orders to move vehicles at night. As the cordon was going into place around 3 a.m., the QRT informed the CO that they were held up because a bridge had been destroyed and they could not cross over. When the CO passed on this information to Leena, her face fell as she was very worried that the boy would die. Finally, they were able to get a chopper evacuation at first light and the boy survived. During the entire night, Leena was beside the stretcher checking on his vital parameters as well as changing his saline intravenous drips. They were literally down to the last bottle by the time the chopper arrived. The CO stated that it was entirely due

to her selfless devotion and professionalism that the boy
survived.

The CO went on to say that the men were totally
devoted to Leena as they were witness to her total and
selfless dedication to them, her courage under fire and
the limits she would go towards ensuring their well-being
and survival.

On 26 January 1994, Captain Leena was awarded
the Sena Medal for gallantry in combat. The Corps
Commander who had finally allowed her to move to the
Valley had now become the Army Chief, and it was his
pleasant duty to present Captain Leena with her award for
gallantry at the Army Day parade in Delhi on 15 January
1995.

The Army Chief remembered Leena and the part they
had both played in this episode when he was her Corps
Commander.

While awarding her the medal, he said, 'Congratulations,
Leena. I am glad we took the right decision. Well done!
The Army is proud of you.'

Leena said, 'Thank you, Sir,' and was happy that the
Chief remembered her name and the incident.

A year later, the Colonel of the Regiment received a
telephone call from Captain Leena, inviting him to her
wedding. After conveying her invitation, she added, 'Sir, I
have to thank you on many counts, but I am most grateful to
you for allowing me to remain with the battalion despite the
pressure at all levels to prevent me from going with them to
the Valley. Thanks to you, I am now wedded to the battalion
in more ways than one, because I am happy to inform you,
Sir, that I am marrying the adjutant of the battalion.'

The general was pleasantly surprised and said, 'I am delighted to hear this good news, Leena, particularly in the choice of the man you wish to marry. Please accept my congratulations, but tell me, how did this happen?'

Leena replied with a laugh. 'That, Sir, is another story!'

Postscript

Captain Leena made history, just as the Colonel of the Regiment had predicted. She is the first lady medical officer of the Indian Army to be posted to an all-male infantry battalion as its regimental medical officer. Further, she is also the first woman of the Indian Army to serve under fire and to be awarded a medal for gallantry in actual combat conditions.

On completion of five years of service, Captain Leena opted to leave the Army. She went on to specialize in oncology and now works with a renowned hospital in Delhi. She and her husband have two children.

Jai! Jai Singh!

A promise is a promise

A man limped out of the porch of Pune railway station and blinked in the sudden glare of the outside sun. He was using a crutch and found it difficult to handle his wheeled suitcase and walk at the same time.

His eyes lit up when he saw a military ambulance parked near the porch. He approached the driver and asked if he could get a lift to the Artificial Limb Centre (ALC), explaining that he was a disabled Army veteran. The driver relieved him of his bag and said he was from the ALC and would be glad to take him there.

The ALC is a home away from home for thousands of soldiers from the Indian Army who have lost limbs in war. It is located close to the Command Hospital in Pune, which provides beds for these disabled veterans in spacious barracks that are over 150 years old. Ancient trees bring nature close to the windows of the patients. The pace of rehabilitation is unhurried, and this gives amputees time to overcome the trauma of losing a limb and cope with an uncertain future.

Disabled soldiers are required to revisit the ALC from time to time for the manufacture or repair of their artificial limbs. On one such visit, about a decade after retirement, an officer was walking towards the workshop at the ALC to check on the repair of his artificial limb. On the way, he saw a man on crutches standing under a tree. It was the same man who had arrived the previous day at the railway station.

'Ram, Ram Sahib,' the man said.

The officer greeted him in return but could not quite remember who the man was. He wondered whether he was a soldier he had met somewhere in the course of his service or at the ALC itself, or someone who was just being respectful and polite. So he smiled, wished him in return and carried on.

The next day, on his walk to the workshop, the officer saw the man again. He was standing in the same place. This time, the man smiled and came forward. 'Ram, Ram Sahib,' he said and added, 'Sahib does not remember me.' The officer, who was a retired general, stopped. They shook hands. The man said that he was a naik (corporal) from the 16th Light Cavalry and that he had driven the general around his unit many years earlier.

The 16th Light Cavalry is the oldest armoured regiment in the Indian Army. The composition of its troops is from the southern states of Tamil Nadu, Kerala and Andhra Pradesh. The regiment had fought well during the Burma campaign, winning the maximum number of battle honours among all Indian tank regiments during World War II. Field Marshal Slim accorded it the honour of taking the surrender of the opposing armoured regiment that had fought against them. At the surrender ceremony, the Japanese Colonel stated that his regiment was glad to surrender to the 16th Light Cavalry because they had fought like tigers and were, therefore, most worthy of receiving their samurai¹ swords.

After exchanging a few pleasantries, the officer asked the soldier his name. 'Jai Singh, Sahib,' he replied.

The officer raised his eyebrows and said, 'That's a strange name for a soldier from south India! Jai Singh is a north Indian name. How did you get this name?'

The soldier smiled, showing an even set of white teeth. He was dark, well-built, tall and handsome. He was dressed in the blue-and-white-striped military hospital clothes, which are standard issue to all soldiers who are patients at military hospitals, all over India. Both of them were waiting to be called up for the measurement and repair of their artificial limbs, and both had time on their hands. In response to the officer's question, the soldier smiled and said, 'Long story, Sahib.'

The general looked around and saw an empty bench under a tree. Benches dotted the layout of the ALC, permitting soldiers to sit around as they waited. The general and the soldier walked towards the bench and sat down.

The soldier began his story. Apparently, he believed all stories began with the words, 'Once upon a time.' He was comfortable with English. Although not entirely fluent, he could nonetheless express himself quite well.

'Once upon a time,' he began, 'my grandfather was fighting in Burma during World War II. He had become very close friends with another soldier named Jai Singh. Both were part of a medium machine gun detachment of their battalion that was supporting an infantry brigade, which was struggling to beat back the Japanese at the Battle of Kohima.'

The soldier was referring to a battle that would eventually turn the tide in the battle for Burma.[2]

The Japanese had reached Kohima, which was a gateway to India from the north-east and is today the capital of Nagaland. A historic battle was fought there, with objectives captured, lost, recaptured and lost, and won again. This battle had important possible outcomes. If the Japanese won, India would be open to the Japanese Army. If the Allies won, it would mean a hard slog back into Burma to wrest it back from the Japanese and then on to Malaya, Singapore, Siam (now Thailand) and the Dutch East Indies.

The soldier continued with the story as narrated to him by his grandfather, whose name was Mohan Chander.

'It was during one of these battles that Grandfather's friend Jai Singh got wounded. A piece of shrapnel from a mortar bomb ripped open his abdomen during one of the Japanese counter-attacks. Two members of the detachment carried Jai Singh away. My grandfather had to carry on with beating back the counter-attack, manning the machine gun on his own. After the attack had petered out, he went looking for Jai Singh and found him lying in the open. He was beyond help. There was nothing that my grandfather could do except apply a first-field dressing on Jai Singh's abdomen to keep the contents inside.

'Grandfather lifted Jai Singh into his arms and took him to the shade of a tree. Jai Singh opened his eyes and said, "I knew you would come." He had lost a lot of blood and had become very weak. After a long silence, he told Grandfather that just a few days earlier, he had received mail from home. The letter had been written two months earlier. His wife could not write, and the letter had been penned by the local schoolteacher so nothing personal could be conveyed. She had, however, managed to convey to her husband that she prayed daily at the temple for his safe return.

'Jai Singh smiled ruefully and said that could no longer happen. He would never return. My grandfather tried to assure him that professional medical help was on the way and he would soon be well again.

'Jai Singh looked at my grandfather and said, "We both know that I will not survive. It will be good if you remain with me until the end. I don't want to go away alone."

'After a while, he said, "It will be nice if you could visit my wife after this war is over and tell her that my last thoughts were of her. Tell her that I am sorry it had to end this way, but there was nothing I could do about it. Please do what you can for her. Please see that she gets her family pension." He was silent for a while, and Grandfather thought he was about to lose him, but Jai Singh had only closed his eyes because he was in great pain.

'After a while, he continued, "It would have been nice if we had a son. He would have looked after my wife. Now that I will be gone, there will be no one to take care of her and to continue my bloodline. With me, my name will die." He sighed and closed his eyes once again.

'My grandfather kept quiet for some time and then said, "Jai, I would like to assure you that your wife will be

cared for as though she is part of my own family. If my wife
and I have a son, we will name him Jai Singh. If we have a
daughter, we will call her Jaya."

'Jai Singh smiled. He was getting weaker by the
moment. "Thank you," he whispered. A little while later,
he was gone. Jai Singh had joined his forefathers and his
God. For him, the war was over, but he had not been able
to live to tell the tale. Grandfather decided to sit with Jai
Singh's body till the stretcher-bearers arrived.

'Meanwhile, the battle raged on around them. While
Grandfather was waiting, the Japanese launched a strong
barrage. Artillery shells and mortar bombs fell through
what was left of the forest canopy, throwing up mounds of
earth and splintering the rocky hillside.

'Grandfather had to leave Jai Singh and hurry back
through the curtain of black smoke and fires caused
by the incendiary Japanese bombs. He was just in time
to stop a platoon of Japanese soldiers from attacking
his position. *"Banzai! Banzai!"* they yelled as they charged
at Grandfather's platoon locality. Grandfather and his
comrades waited till the Japanese came really close and
then opened up with their machine guns, mowing them
down. Many died. A few, who got through, died on the
barbed wire entanglement protecting their position, and
the rest went back. It was a full two hours before the
Japanese attacks finally petered out, and Grandfather was
able to go back to Jai Singh.

'There was a full moon that night, and the moonlight
shone through what was left of the leaves of the trees. The
light and shade made a filigree pattern on Jai Singh's face
as he lay peacefully at the base of a tree. It looked as though

he was fast asleep. After a while, the stretcher-bearers came along with some mules to take away the wounded and the dead. Grandfather helped load Jai Singh's body on to one of the mules. He watched the mule take away his best friend. They had gone some distance when suddenly, the shelling recommenced. A mortar bomb landed close to the mules and they stampeded in panic. Grandfather could see Jai Singh's body bouncing on top of one of the mules as they ran away. That was the last that Grandfather saw of his friend. He felt very sad that this was the way it had to end.

'That night, Grandfather returned to his trench, which he had shared with Jai Singh. Jai Singh's possessions amounted to all that was contained in his backpack. There was a threadbare blanket, a rain cape, a pair of worn-out PT shoes, a change of uniform, his toiletries and a few letters. His wallet contained a few rupee notes and a photograph of his wife, who appeared to be little more than a girl. Jai Singh had told Grandfather that her name was Rukmini.

'Whenever Grandfather and Jai Singh could talk during lulls in the battle, they would speak about their families and the future they hoped to see if they survived the war. Both wanted children and both wanted a girl and a boy. The thought of going back home and raising a family was what sustained them both during the darkest hours of the Battle of Kohima.

'Jai Singh, however, was now dead and all his dreams had died with him.

'Grandfather repacked Jai Singh's belongings. He had barely done this when the clatter of machine guns and the thump of mortars called him to beat back another Japanese attack.

'In one of the many attacks and counter-attacks that were launched by the Japanese and the Allies, Grandfather was also wounded and had to be evacuated from the battlefield. For him, too, the war was over, but he would live to carry out his promise to Jai Singh.

'World War II ended in Europe on 8 May 1945, but the war in the East lingered on until 14 August, the same year.

'It took some time before my grandfather and grandmother could finally visit Rukmini, Jai Singh's wife. By this time, my father had already been born. My father was named Jai Singh, as promised. The three of them went to meet Rukmini in her village in Rajasthan.

'Rukmini was alone, and she was glad to see my grandparents. She and my father, who was only a very small baby, got on very well. Grandfather and Grandmother, who lived in a village in Velachery, a district in Tamil Nadu, invited Rukmini to make her home with them but she refused. She preferred to stay alone with the memories of her husband. My grandparents, however, visited Rukmini every year when Grandfather got his annual leave. He did all the paperwork for her family pension and made sure that it came to her on time.

'One day, while they were at Rukmini's home, she spoke wistfully of the past. They were sitting in the *angan* (courtyard). It was a clear full moon night. She said, "Every morning I used to go to the temple to pray for my husband's safe return. It was difficult living alone, and I constantly worried about his safety. At night, I used to sit here in the angan and look up at the sky and wonder whether he, too, was also looking at the same moon and the stars and whether he was also thinking of me.

'"During the day, I used to wait for the postman in the hope of receiving a letter from my husband—the red-and-grey forces letter—that came all too rarely through the Army Post Office. The postman was a kind man. He used to read my husband's letters to me. My husband knew about this, so nothing much could be said in his letters, but I could understand his underlying concern for me.

'"And then came the day of that terrible telegram that told me that my husband was no more. The postman read it out to me. It began with those dreadful words: *We regret to inform you that* . . . Words that no Army wife should ever hear! At first, I could not comprehend what he was saying, and when I did, my whole world came crashing down. Everything became dark and dismal. God had failed me. Why couldn't He have saved him? Why did my husband have to die so that others might live? I asked these questions of God again and again, but I received no answer.

'"My husband and I wanted children. We would have liked to have had a boy and a girl. How nice that would have been! But God and the war willed it otherwise. Why do we have wars? Why can't people live without fighting with each other? Why can't we be allowed to carry on with our lives and live in peace?"

'My grandparents had no answers for these difficult questions. My grandfather said they just remained quiet and let Rukmini get it off her chest. Then Rukmini began to cry. My infant father seemed to understand that something was amiss and crawled on to her lap. Rukmini clasped him to her chest. Rukmini and the baby both seemed to give comfort to each other and thus began a relationship that was to last forever.

'My father, Jai Singh, as a young child, became very fond of Rukmini. He was taught to call Rukmini *'mataji'* (mother) and a mother–son relationship developed between them. Grandmother and Rukmini also became very close friends. The birth of Jai Singh was followed by the birth of a girl. My parents named her Jaya. My grandfather's promise to his friend was now complete. My father and his sister were lucky to have two mothers.'

The officer who had quietly listened to the story, however, had a question to ask. He said, 'Your grandfather kept his promise by naming your father Jai Singh, but how is it that you too are named Jai Singh?'

Jai Singh drew himself up proudly, stood and answered, 'Sir, my father is Jai Singh; I am Jai Singh; my son is Jai Singh! There will always be a Jai Singh in our family!'

Postscript

Jai Singh the Second, the narrator of this story, settled in Velachery, Tamil Nadu, and Jai Singh the Third has joined the 16th Light Cavalry, his father's regiment, the oldest cavalry regiment in the Indian Army. He, like many others in the Indian Army, carries on the tradition of successive generations following in the footsteps of their fathers.

Jai Singh the Fourth was born recently. India's destiny will rest on the shoulders of his generation. Our country's security will be in good hands as long as their forefathers' values live on in them.

The Bent Bayonet

Simplicity, bravery, loyalty—hallmarks of the Indian soldier

It is a custom of units of the Indian Army in peace stations to leave their barracks once a year and go out into the countryside to do what is known as 'collective training'. This entails spending two to three months in the jungles, plains or mountainside of the country, depending on where the unit is likely to relocate for its next operational stint. The advantage of such training is that, because it takes place away from civilization, it is uninterrupted, and all commanders up and down the chain of command have the opportunity to train their commands effectively and to their satisfaction.

It was some time after India became independent that it was the turn of one such unit from a Sikh regiment to carry out collective training in the month of March. The unit was scheduled to move to the jungles of north-east India, and so it was decided that they go to the forests of Shivpuri near Gwalior for their collective training.

The battalion liaised with the Forest Department for permission to train in the forest near Shivpuri. The Forest Department agreed that the battalion could train in the forest provided they took every precaution against forest fires and took care of the ecology. The Forest Department was particularly concerned about the safety of the tiger population. They felt that the presence of the military would work as a deterrent to poaching by local 'shikaris', which was endemic even in those days.

The battalion left Gwalior soon after permission was received, moved into the forest near Shivpuri and commenced training. The training was in harmony with the forest and its wildlife, and all went well for a while.

Sometime later, the forest warden informed the Commanding Officer (CO) that they had moved into an area frequented by tigers and cautioned the men to be careful. He mentioned that tigers do not normally attack humans unless they feel threatened; therefore, on no account should the soldiers attempt to kill a tiger unless they were attacked and it was a life-threatening situation.

The matter was discussed at length by the CO and his men, and a solution was finally worked out. It was decided that only one person from each company would be permitted to have ammunition in the magazine of his rifle. It was also decided that it would be the company subedar who would thus be armed to take care of life-threatening situations, and he would use his discretion and only fire as a last resort. The battalion's training continued peacefully. After a while, however, it was decided that there was a need to conduct tactical training of the sub-units, and a larger area was required. The unit, therefore, struck camp and moved deeper into the jungle. The forest officer was informed of the battalion's new location.

The battalion commenced its tactical training in the new area and came across many wild animals, including tigers, during their manoeuvres. However, there was neither danger nor cause for alarm.

After a while, the forest warden came to meet the CO. He was guided to the new location by one of the unit's company quartermaster havildars, who was located in the battalion's rear administrative echelon.

The forest officer informed the CO that he had received information from the forest people that the *fauji* (army) camp was close to the beat of a tiger and that the men needed to be particularly alert.

The CO was not particularly perturbed. In fact, he was happy that the men would be tested against a live threat and, therefore, would learn to be more alert and controlled. He did not change his orders and reiterated his earlier order that, except for the company subedar, the men would not be given any ammunition.

On the evening of 16 March 1954, the CO was sitting outside the officers' mess tent having a cup of tea, when he heard loud shouts from one of the soldiers who was about 200 yards away. The man was shouting, '*Kha liya, kha liya, bachao, bachao*', which in effect means 'I have been bitten, save me, save me!'

The CO picked up his walking stick and ran towards the man who was shouting along with some of the other men who were working nearby. They saw a soldier, Sepoy Fauja Singh, grappling with a tiger!

All the men shouted, '*Aa gaye, aa gaye* (We are coming, we are coming!)' and then the battalion war cry, '*Bole So Nihal, Sat Sri Akal*'. The tiger, seeing the men running towards it, bounded off with Fauja Singh's turban in its mouth. Fauja Singh was found to be badly mauled by the tiger during this encounter and had to be evacuated and admitted to Jhansi Military Hospital, where he was treated for his wounds.

The CO was now in a quandary. The safety of his men was his primary responsibility; however, he also knew that as long as the soldiers were in the forest, they were also protectors of the forest and all its bird and animal life.

There was, however, no question of stopping his men's training merely because there was a tiger in the vicinity of his camp! He called for a small meeting of his Company Commanders and reiterated that this was an ideal opportunity for the men and their Commanders to exercise restraint, fire discipline and courage in the face of danger. The senior subedar asked the CO whether the men could now be issued ammunition. The CO turned down his request, saying that their aim should not be to kill the tiger but only to drive it away. However, he allowed the men to 'fix bayonets' on their rifles to help them feel a little more secure and the training could carry on as usual.

The .303 Lee Enfield Mk III rifle was a very robust bolt-action rifle with a wooden butt and stock. It had a magazine that housed five rounds, and after each round was fired, the soldier was required to move the bolt with his right hand. This movement of the bolt resulted in extracting the case of the fired round, ejecting it and pushing another round into the chamber to allow the shooter to fire the next round. The bayonet was fixed with a catch at the muzzle of the rifle.

Training carried on as usual. A few days later, the tiger once again entered the camp area in the morning. The soldiers raised an alarm, and with all the shouting and noise, the tiger ran away and disappeared into the undergrowth. The CO immediately called his Company Commanders and instructed them on organizing a 'beat' to drive the tiger away by getting into a semi-circle and shouting and beating utensils so as to create a lot of noise, which would drive the tiger away. He briefed them on exactly how this had to be done and also what the men had to do in case the tiger pounced on any of them. He demonstrated how the men should take the tiger on their bayonet if any of them were attacked, and how the remainder needed to go to the rescue of their comrade with their bayonets.

That very evening, the tiger returned to the camp area, growling and roaring, before dashing back into the jungle. The men quickly formed a semi-circle, organizing a 'beat' and approaching the area where the tiger was last seen. The men shouted their war cry, '*Bole So Nihal*,' and approached the dense undergrowth into which the tiger had disappeared.

There was no sign of the tiger for a while, but the men continued to push forward, shouting and making a noise, when suddenly the tiger leapt from the undergrowth with an angry roar. It jumped at the outermost man of the semi-circle of the beat from a distance of about ten to fifteen yards. The man at the receiving end was Sepoy Sucha Singh, who was the junior-most soldier in the company. He was kept at the outermost fringe because of his lack of experience. Sepoy Sucha Singh was indeed a simple soldier with just a year of service, but he did not forget the orders of his CO. Displaying cool courage and steel nerves, he took the tiger on his bayonet, but fell down with the weight of this huge animal on top of him. The tiger was now motionless, and except for part of his turban, Sucha Singh could not be seen, but there was a great deal of blood oozing from below the tiger's body. One could not make out whether the blood was from the tiger or from Sepoy Sucha Singh. In the meantime, the other soldiers ran forward and also used their bayonets on the wounded tiger. But the tiger was dead. Sucha Singh's bayonet had gone straight into the tiger's heart.

Sucha Singh, however, was pinned down with the weight of the tiger on him, and he was covered in blood. It took twelve strong men to lift the tiger off Sucha Singh. It transpired that the blood was the tiger's and that Sucha Singh was unhurt. As soon as he was pulled out from under the tiger, Sucha Singh picked up his turban and started shouting, '*Oye! Meri rifle le gayi* (Oh! The tiger has taken my rifle)'. He was told to stop shouting and not to be foolish. The tiger was lying there dead in front of him and his rifle was safe. Sucha Singh's rifle was pulled out from the body of the tiger. The bayonet, which had a ten-inch blade, had gone straight into the body of the tiger and into its heart, getting bent in the process. Bayonets are made of the best quality tempered steel, and to have got bent is an indication of how much pressure was exerted by the weight of the tiger on the bayonet and on Sucha Singh.

Sucha Singh, simple soldier that he was, felt happy that his rifle was safe and that he had not let down his CO, whose orders he had followed in letter and spirit.

Later, when the Brigade Commander met Sepoy Sucha Singh, he was asked what had happened and who had really killed the tiger. He replied in typical rustic Punjabi, '*Sahibji, sherni mari tan mere* bayonet *naal hi hai, par jadon thalle gir gayi pher tere mere warge kai* bayonet *maran lag paye!* (Sir, the tigress actually got killed with my bayonet, but when it fell down, then every Tom, Dick and Harry also pushed in their bayonets).' The Brigade Commander had a good laugh and gave immediate orders for Sucha Singh to be promoted to lance naik for his courage, discipline and presence of mind.

The turban of Sepoy Fauja Singh was recovered from the lair of the tigress. Along with it, the men discovered two tiger cubs. It now became clear that the tigress was only trying to protect her cubs, and the men felt bad that the tigress had died valiantly trying to save her cubs from what she thought was a threat to their existence.

Fauja Singh's turban was sent to him at the hospital, along with a message about what had transpired since the day that the tigress had first attacked him.

The forest officer was also notified, and the tiger cubs were handed over to the Forest Department. An application was made to the Forest Department for the retention of the skin, which was granted in due course. The skin, after initial local curing, was sent to Van Ingens, who were world-famous taxidermists in Bangalore, and was later sent back to the unit after being properly cured.

The story made it to the local newspapers in Agra, and Sucha Singh, now a lance naik, became a sort of local hero within the district. More importantly, there was much appreciation for the discipline of the soldiers of the 17th Battalion of the Sikh Regiment, who had followed the orders of their CO even at grave risk to their own lives and had acted beyond fear.

As far as the battalion was concerned, bravery and courage were displayed not only by Sucha Singh, Fauja Singh and the soldiers who faithfully followed the orders of their CO, but also by the tigress who defended her young ones at the cost of her own life.

The courage of Sepoy Sucha Singh was widely acclaimed, as were the steadfastness and discipline of the soldiers of this unit of the Sikh Regiment.

In recognition of the bravery of the tigress and the courage, discipline, steadiness and resilience of the men, the 17th Battalion of the Sikh Regiment earned the sobriquet 'Tiger Paltan', by which name it is still known.

Postscript

This is probably the only incident where a full-grown tigress was killed by a soldier wielding a bayonet. If you ever visit the officers' mess of the 17th Battalion of the Sikh Regiment, you will see the skin of this tigress and, by its side, the bent bayonet on one of its walls.

It's Never Too Late

*The sky is the limit for others; that is where the
Indian Air Force begins*

This is the story of an Indian Air Force (IAF) pilot, Squadron Leader A.B. Devayya (Tubby Devayya), who took off on a mission from an airbase in north India during the 1965 Indo–Pak War and never returned. In the Indian Armed Forces, such persons are first listed as 'Missing in action' and after a court of inquiry and a laid-down time of seven years, they are declared 'Missing in action—believed killed'.[1]

In 1965, India was still in the process of reorganizing its armed forces after the debacle of the Sino–Indian War of 1962. Pakistan, on the other hand, had received massive military aid from the United States. This completely upset the relative strength between India and Pakistan. Aware of now having the upper hand, Pakistan decided it was the ideal opportunity to go to war with India to annex the state of Jammu and Kashmir.

Without a formal declaration of war, Pakistan seized the initiative and attacked Indian airfields on the evening of 6 September 1965. Indian fighter and bomber aircraft on the ground at these airfields were caught in the open, and twenty-one aircraft were destroyed—a loss that India could ill afford. What the IAF learnt later, with the capture of downed Pakistan Air Force (PAF) pilots, was that Pakistan had been preparing for such an offensive air operation since March that year.

That evening, news began trickling in to the pilots at Indian airfields that the PAF had destroyed a large number of Indian aircraft on the ground. This destruction of our aircraft without a declaration of war angered many Indian armed forces personnel, and Squadron Leader Tubby Devayya was one of the most incensed.

Devayya had joined the No. 1 Squadron on 31 August 1965 in Adampur, just before the onset of the war. Tubby was a rough and tough fighter pilot from Coorg; he was also a talented hockey player. His game on the field showcased his outstanding qualities of skill, determination, persistence and the will to win. He was commissioned on 6 November 1954 and initially flew Vampires. He was an instructor at the Air Force Flying College in Hakimpet when, during the outbreak of hostilities, he volunteered for front-line service. His request was accepted, and he was attached to the No. 1 Squadron in Adampur.

As dusk fell on the evening of 6 September 1965, the pilots of No. 1 Squadron in Adampur, who were waiting to go into action, were told to return to the officers' mess and await orders. The officers got on to their motorbikes and rode back to the mess in pitch darkness because a 'blackout' had been enforced not only at the base but across all of Punjab.

Orders from the IAF Command Headquarters went out late on the night of 6 September to Adampur and Halwara for the Mystere and Hunter squadrons to plan strikes against PAF airbases. Western Air Command directed the Commanding Officer (CO) of the No. 1

Squadron—'The Adampur Tigers'—to respond to the PAF attack. The CO opted for an attack by his squadron on the Pakistani airfield at Sargodha.

The squadron was to launch an attack at dawn on 7 September. Time over target (TOT) was 5.55 a.m. Indian Standard Time (IST), which was fifteen minutes before sunrise in Pakistan Standard Time (PKT). The given TOT, therefore, gave barely enough light for the recognition of targets. The planners had erroneously chosen the Adampur sunrise time of 0555 hours rather than Sargodha, where sunrise would take place only at 0610 hours, due to the fact that sunrise time increases as one flies further west. Since the aircraft would be flying at high speed, it would still be dark at Sargodha when the Mysteres would be over their targets.

The CO, Wing Commander Taneja, asked for the TOT to be delayed by fifteen minutes to 0610 hours. But as the Hunter squadron from Halwara was already tasked with a strike on the same target at that time, the TOT for the No. 1 Squadron could not be changed. Taneja would therefore be attacking his targets in the dark.

Devayya remained enraged at the destruction of so many Indian aircraft on the ground and he was itching to confront the enemy. However, because he was surplus to the squadron at Adampur, he was placed in reserve and detailed as a standby, which meant that he would participate in the raid only if one of the aircraft raiding Sargodha could not get airborne. The fact that he was a 'reserve' troubled him even more, as it put a question mark on whether he would be given a shot at fighting the enemy.

Sargodha was at the extreme range of the Mysteres, with a flight time of thirty minutes from Adampur. The entire operation was estimated to take one hour. Being on the outer limits of the Mystere's range, no tactical re-routing was possible, nor could the aircraft be permitted the luxury of taking on other targets. No allowance was available for air combat manoeuvres, as even a simple air combat manoeuvre would guzzle up valuable fuel. They could only limit themselves to a single attack run over their targets before returning to the base at Adampur.

The pilots knew they would be attacking their targets the next day. However, only Wing Commander Taneja knew that Sargodha was the target. The rest were not privy to the where and when of their mission. While they were still in the officers' mess, orders were received that the pilots of the No. 1 Squadron were to have an early dinner and catch up on sleep. That meant an early morning mission, but no further information was given.

The pilots slept fitfully that night and were woken up by their civilian orderlies at 0300 hours and told to report to the squadron briefing room at 0400 hours. No mission details were given, and they could only guess that it was something important.

The twelve pilots and the two standbys, wearing their Mystere g-suits, assembled at the briefing room at 0400 hours when most of India was still asleep. Tubby Devayya was among them, as he was one of the reserves. They crowded around the black wooden board, which displayed the pilots' names, aircraft numbers, armament loads, start-up time, wheel roll time, TOT, fuel states and watch synchronization time. The blackout curtains had been drawn to prevent any light from showing. An air photograph of the Sargodha base, taken by the photo reconnaissance (PR) Canberra aircraft in 1958, indicated that they would be attacking Sargodha.

The Sargodha complex consisted of four airfields: Sargodha Main, Chota Sargodha to the west, Wagowal to the north and Bagtanwala to the east. The network of airfields was located across the river Chenab, with the Kirana Hills rising 1500 feet to the south-east. Sargodha Main was the target for No. 1 Squadron.

Wing Commander 'Omi' Taneja, the Squadron Commander, commenced the briefing at 0415 hours. Taneja's demeanour was sober, but his body language was cool and upbeat, and the pilots could sense that he meant to go all out to ensure the success of his plan. His voice did not display any trace of anxiety, and there was no doubt that he was a man who knew exactly how the raid was to be carried out, that he was in charge and that he would not accept any half-hearted effort from anyone. He outlined the plan of attack:

'Our target is the heavily guarded PAF airbase at Sargodha (Main). As you can see from your maps, the Sargodha airfield is 300 miles inside Pakistan. Our attack will be launched with twelve aircraft in three waves. I will lead the attack with the first wave. The four aircraft of my formation will each be armed with 8 x T-10 rockets. The second wave of four aircraft will be led by Squadron Leader 'Danny' Satur. The aircraft of his wave will be armed with 2 x 18 SNEB 68 mm rocket pods. Squadron Leader

Sudarshan Handa will lead the third wave. Handa's four
aircraft will each be armed with 2 x 1000 lb bombs.

'I want to make it clear that you have just enough fuel
to hit your targets and get back. You will not have the luxury
of a second pass over the target area, so make sure you
keep your eyes open and access your targets as you go in.
Your priority is enemy aircraft on the ground; next are the
installations that you must have seen on the photograph
pinned up on the board. There could be differences, as
that is an old photograph. Visibility will not be too good,
but I will not accept that as an excuse. The success of the
raid will depend on the number of enemy aircraft and vital
installations destroyed.

'I am reminding you once again to have a clear
understanding that time, fuel and distance limit your
ability to destroy your targets and get back. No frills are
required.'

Wing Commander Taneja then briefed them as to how
they would take off.

'You will start up and taxi out to the take-off point in
the sequence that I have given you, in total radio silence and
on unlit taxi tracks. The runway lights will come on when
the aircraft are ready to roll, starting with mine. Take-off
will be in pairs, with each aircraft occupying one half of the
runway. The intervals between pairs will be thirty seconds
to avoid the jet wake of the aircraft in front. You have been
taught this a hundred times, so I don't expect any problems
at the start of our mission!

'We will take off at 0528 hours, and the fly-in will be
at 300 feet above ground level. This will be in darkness,

so keep your eyes open for the aircraft in front of you. The time to reach our targets is thirty minutes. We will attack our targets at thirty-second intervals, beginning at 0558 hours just as dawn will be breaking over our targets. Navigation will take place only by compass and stopwatch, as the darkness will not permit map reading. After carrying out the raid, the altitude on our return will be 50 feet to avoid enemy radar.

'Are there any questions?'

There were no questions, but the tension and excitement were palpable. This was the 'real thing'. Most of the pilots were very young, and this was going to be their first operational mission. Although the team was apprehensive about being able to perform during actual combat, they felt empowered by Wing Commander Taneja's supreme confidence in their competence. All the pilots listened to the briefing in silence, visualizing the plan as it unfolded. Their faces were a study in concentrated attention.

'All right then,' Taneja said. 'Best of luck and see you when we get back.'

As the target was at the extreme endurance of the Mystere, the pilots understood and accepted that there was no scope for attacking additional targets or deviating from the specified route, and that top priority was to be given to enemy aircraft spotted on the runway. Two senior flying instructors were on standby in case any of the twelve aircraft dropped out.

One of the standbys was Squadron Leader Devayya. Flying Officer Philip Rajkumar was placed in the last wave

of four aircraft and nominated as 'Tail-end Charlie'. Enemy
aircraft attempting to intercept the attack would have to
approach from the rear so as to bring their forward-firing
guns to bear on Taneja's attacking aircraft. The job of 'Tail-
end Charlie' was to warn the others of any impending
danger; it required the keen eyes of a hawk and a 'rubber
neck' to look as far back as possible.

The aircraft technicians and armourers had worked
around the clock during the night of 6 September
preparing the Mysteres for the attack. They wheeled out
the aircraft from their protective pens in the early hours of
7 September. They felt responsible and accountable for the
effective performance of their respective aircraft as there
is a close, unwritten bond between them, their aircraft and
the pilots. Having carried out all the necessary checks, they
were now wiping off the night's dew from their respective
fighter jets. The emblem of the head of a roaring tiger on
the front part of the fuselage of each Mystere of the No. 1
Squadron symbolized the ferocity with which the 'tigers'
would carry out their mission.

As the pilots were walking towards their aircraft in
the cool morning air, an air raid 'red' siren (warning for
an imminent attack) went off, but it was only a passing
satellite and no enemy aircraft appeared overhead.

The squadron of twelve aircraft formed up in a stream
of three sections of four Mysteres each. There was just
enough starlight for the pilots to guide their aircraft from
their shelters to the runway.

The aircraft technicians and armourers lined up to
wave the pilots on to their targets. This was their mission

too, and they felt responsible for the performance of their planes and their pilots. They waved them off with a silent prayer that they accomplish their mission successfully and return safely.

The sound of twelve jet engines revving up shattered the early morning silence, and the red-hot exhausts of the afterburners pinpointed each aircraft's position in the pre-dawn darkness. Wing Commander Taneja switched on his navigation lights when he was ready, and the control tower responded by switching on the runway lights. There was no communication from the control tower or the pilots due to the strict radio silence being observed. The reserve pilots with the Mysteres that had been borrowed from the No. 32 Squadron (the adjoining squadron) were standing by with their engines running. The reserves were to take off only if any of the twelve designated aircraft aborted their flights.

After the second wave of four aircraft had rolled, Squadron Leader Sudarshan Handa and his wingman, Flight Lieutenant Brar, took to the runway. Behind them were Flight Lieutenant Kahai and Flying Officer P. Rajkumar. After Handa and Brar rolled, one of the standby aircraft suddenly moved on to the runway and started rolling behind Handa. This was Squadron Leader Tubby Devayya.

Devayya had jumped the gun and had already got airborne. He just could not wait to confront the enemy. However, on taking off, one of the pilots of the first wave found that his drop tanks were not feeding into the main fuel line and had to abort. Devayya could now legitimately join the squadron as a designated aircraft had aborted.

As a young flying officer, Tubby had worked hard to master the art and science of air combat. He was motivated by the stories of Indian pilots of the Royal Air Force who had fought with distinction in both World Wars and the 1947–48 Indo–Pak War. His competence was recognized, and in due course, he was appointed as a qualified flying instructor at the Air Force Academy. He used the knowledge and experience gained from conversations with IAF fighter pilots from earlier wars to teach his students the basics of aerial combat. He taught them to be ingenious and innovative so as to get the better of their opponents, stimulating the imagination of his student pilots when narrating these stories to them.

For many years, Tubby Devayya was waiting for an opportunity to get at the enemy so that he could put into practice his ideas on aerial combat and exercise his skills. This was the opportunity he was waiting for, and he had decided that, come what may, he was not going to be denied the opportunity to get to grips with the enemy. When faced with the problem of the non-availability of aircraft for the reserve pilots of No. 1 Squadron, Wing Commander Taneja managed to get two Mysteres from No. 32 Squadron located on the same airfield. Tubby was allotted one of them.

Squadron Leader Devayya ended up at the tail end of the second wave, as Wing Commander Taneja took his aircraft at treetop level to avoid being detected on the PAF radar.

The roar of the jets of Taneja's flight, so close to the ground, woke up sleepy villagers all along the flight path on both sides of the border. The villagers knew that Pakistan and India were at war, and in a way, they were going to be part of the action.

Navigation was by instruments and dead reckoning, which is a technique of mentally calculating an aircraft's position. Five minutes before TOT, the Mysteres led by Wing Commander Taneja were detected by PAF radar.

It was still half-light at Sargodha and much darker than anticipated. Its fighters on combat air patrol (CAP) for airfield defence went on alert, but before they could react, Taneja and his aircraft were already over the Sargodha airfield.

Although Sargodha had readied a CAP of two Sabres and a Starfighter, the first inkling of the IAF's arrival was the sound of the Mysteres pulling up to deliver their attack. Taneja's raid was met with complete surprise on the airfield. 'The first we knew about the raid was when we heard the thunder of rockets, followed by the stutter of cannon,' recollects Group Captain Zafar Masud, Station Commander, Sargodha.

The Mysteres came roaring over even as the defending anti-aircraft (ack-ack) guns started firing. IAF Canberras had attacked Sargodha the previous night, and more raids were expected but perhaps not so early in the morning when it was still dark. If the visibility conditions were poor for the defenders, they were equally bad for the attackers.

The Mysteres, led by Wing Commander Taneja, reached the area over the target in Sargodha at 0558 PKT. Taneja pulled up short of Sargodha and led the first dive on to the airfield along with his wingman Verma.

A large, four-engine transport aircraft lying on the runway was attacked with rockets and destroyed. The remainder attacked their technical area, hangars and circular pens. Heavy ack-ack opened up on the attacking aircraft as they pulled up to attack. As Wing Commander Taneja pulled out of his dive, he noticed two Sabres and an F-104 Starfighter parked further on the operational readiness platform (ORP). Taneja then broke radio silence to inform the second wave to attack them.

He radioed, '*Red Leader to Strike Formation, 2 Sabres and one Starfighter on ORP. Engage and destroy.*'

However, the light conditions were too poor for the second wave to see the aircraft indicated by Taneja in time, so they attacked the other targets, including hangars and circular aircraft pens with aircraft in them. One Starfighter was observed burning furiously and was claimed as destroyed.

When Taneja pulled out of his single pass and turned back for the base, Squadron Leader Devayya, the reserve pilot, was at the tail end of the group. He had initially tagged along behind the second wave of four and streamed in over Sargodha just as Taneja had turned around for base. He attacked targets as they were visible to him on the airfield. When the Mysteres 'hit the deck' to head for home, Devayya continued to be at the tail-end of the squadron.

For Tubby Devayya, this action had not been enough.

In the meantime, PAF Starfighters had been alerted by Pakistan's Sakesar radar station. They scrambled at 0555 PKT and were directed towards Sargodha. A Pakistani F-104 Starfighter, flown by Flight Lieutenant Amjad

Hussain, made visual contact with Sargodha after he saw the sky lit up by the PAF ground defences. By the time the Starfighters reached the scene of action, the Mysteres had already exited the airfield and were clear of Sargodha flying at 150–200 mph on a south-easterly heading towards India. Devayya was the last one out of Sargodha and the first one to be spotted by the F-104 Starfighter piloted by Flight Lieutenant Amjad Hussain. The duties of 'Tail End Charlie' had now devolved on Devayya.

None of the 'waves' were witness to the action that followed, so there are varying accounts of what actually happened. Narratives by Air Commodore Kaiser Tufail of Pakistan in *Great Air Battles of the Pakistan Air Force*; by John Fricker in his book *Battle for Pakistan: The Air War of 1965*; by Squadron Leader Rana T.S. Chhina in *The Indian Air Force Memorial Book*; and by P.V.S. Jagan Mohan and Samir Chopra in *The India Pakistan Air War of 1965*, however, throw some light on the air battle between these two fighter pilots.

The Starfighter, piloted by Flight Lieutenant Amjad Hussain, had closed in and got behind the Mystere piloted by Squadron Leader Devayya. Hussain released his Sidewinder missiles that went wide off the mark and landed on the ground. Devayya had two options. First, he could face the Starfighter head-on and fight it out, in which case, even if he survived, he would have no fuel left to fly across the border back to India. The second option was to evade the pursuing Starfighter. The IAF pilots had been instructed not to indulge in personal heroics and instead prioritize the ability to fight again another day. Devayya was, however, of a different breed. Not fighting the enemy was not an option for him. He spotted the interceptor, and instead of carrying on towards home base, he turned around to do battle with the Starfighter, which was a far superior aircraft compared to the Mystere. He probably believed that it was better to fight and die with honour than to turn around and get shot down by a superior aircraft that could have easily caught up with him.

Ignoring the superiority of the Starfighter, Devayya went after Amjad Hussain and began to attack him with unusual ferocity. Hussain used the superior power of the Starfighter in climb and acceleration to lift the combat from ground level to 7000 ft in order to gain more room for manoeuvring. Devayya, however, locked on to the Starfighter and doggedly followed it all the way up, showing considerable courage in doing so because his rate of climb was much slower than the Starfighter. Despite the disparity in the capabilities of his Mystere as compared to the Starfighter, Devayya was determined to close in on the enemy aircraft and destroy it.

Hussain was aware that his advantage in speed would make it difficult to close in on the Mystere in his bid to destroy it, and so he was forced to do a 'yo-yo' (bouncing up and down) to prevent an overshoot and managed to get behind Devayya. He closed in on the Mystere, using his afterburner and, having got Devayya in his sights, fired a burst from the Starfighter's deadly six-barrelled 20-mm Vulcan revolver cannon in a bid to destroy him.

Devayya's Mystere broke to the right and appeared to pass through the deadly stream of bullets, and Hussain broke off the engagement, certain that the stricken Mystere was destroyed. But he did not reckon with Devayya, who was an accomplished and gutsy pilot. Although the Mystere had received several hits, it was not disabled. Devayya had survived the attack and his aircraft was still flyable. There was still a chance to fly back home and if his fuel ran out, he could have ejected safely over Indian territory. Devayya, however, ignored that option. He decided to destroy the Starfighter no matter the odds and went after it.

Devayya once again managed to climb to get behind the Starfighter. Hussain spotted the Mystere when it was turning to get behind him and was under the impression that this was another Mystere that was coming after him after he had destroyed the first one. He was unaware that Devayya had survived his Vulcan onslaught and was now coming after him again. To give himself enough manoeuvring room, Hussain once again pulled up for another yo-yo, bouncing up to 7000 ft and then down to a low level again. As he tried to get behind the Mystere, Hussain realized that he was up against a very determined pilot who was unwilling to give any quarter. The fight continued with Hussain trying every trick to shake off the Mystere with a series of turns, one into the other, developing into a classic 'scissors' manoeuvre. Somehow, Tubby was able to get behind the Starfighter.

At this stage, Hussain made a mistake. He reduced his speed in an attempt to out-turn his determined opponent to deliver the final blow. Although the Starfighter possessed the speed to out-fly any aircraft, it had the limitations of a flying brick in a dogfight. Devayya saw his opportunity, closed in and found the Starfighter in his sights. He pressed home his attack and scored several hits on the Starfighter with his 2 x 30 mm DEFA cannons mounted on either side of the Mystere's fuselage. Amjad now found that his elevator control had frozen due to the cannon strikes from Devayya and lost control. He managed to eject from his stricken aircraft, and his parachute popped just a few hundred feet above the ground.

This was the first and only Mach-2 Starfighter to be destroyed in air combat during the 1965 War. Devayya's successful destruction of a state-of-the-art Starfighter F-104 by a Mystere IV A was an extraordinary feat by any standard.

At Kot Naka village in Pakistan, about five miles south of Pindi Bhattian Tehsil, the farmers were out in the fields about to start their chores when they saw the two aircraft approaching them from the direction of Sargodha. They watched in fascination and awe as the two aircraft wheeled, dived and turned while fighting to get the better of each other. The sound of the aircrafts' cannons reached them, and they wondered how this contest would end. Then suddenly, they saw both aircraft fall out of the sky like leaves from a tree. One of the pilots came down by parachute, and the other aircraft went down across the Jang Canal. The pilot of this aircraft had failed to eject. His body was found intact, thrown clear of the wreckage. He was later buried by the villagers in the fields. It was Squadron Leader Tubby Devayya.

Back in Adampur, an anxious Taneja was waiting for Devayya to join the mission debrief. Everyone was under the impression that Devayya was probably taking his time in the lines of 32 Squadron while returning their borrowed aircraft. After a while, upon inquiring with the 32 Squadron, it was found that Devayya had not returned. Taneja and the rest of the squadron were blissfully unaware of the action fought by Tubby Devayya. With no information from any quarter and an absence of information from anyone, Devayya was eventually listed as 'Missing in action.' Devayya's action would remain lost in the uncertainty of war for years to come.

Wing Commander Taneja proceeded with the debriefing at the conclusion of the mission. Although twelve aircraft took off initially from Adampur, two aircraft of the first wave aborted due to engine problems and the last wave of four aircraft lost its way; initially due to the dust on the runway raised on take-off and then to radio silence, to the darkness and to the fact that the aircraft were not using their navigation lights. Wing Commander Taneja was unhappy with the inability of six aircraft to contribute effectively to the raid. He stated that their performance was unacceptable and he ordered them to attack Sargodha in broad daylight at 0945 hours. This was a tough and dangerous mission because there was no cover of darkness and the alerted defences would give the attackers a hot reception. The chances of being intercepted and shot down were high, but orders were orders and they had to obey.

What followed was another very successful operation, but that's another story.

Declared dead seven years later as per regulations, Devayya would have remained an unsung hero had it not been, ironically, for John Fricker's book *Battle for Pakistan: The Air War of 1965* (published in Pakistan in 1979), which narrated the story of this air battle. It was only in 1980,

a year later and fifteen years after the war, that Group
Captain Taneja, VrC, read John Fricker's account about
the details of Hussain's fight with a 'second' Mystere and
Hussain's own admission of being shot down by an IAF
Mystere over Sargodha on the morning of 7 September
1965. Taneja knew better than anyone else that no other
Mystere pilot had had air combat with a Starfighter that
fateful morning of 7 September 1965. Therefore, there was
no question of there being a 'second' Mystere, and that it
was Devayya who, although stricken, continued to battle
with the Starfighter. Devayya had, in fact, survived the
first volley of bullets and was still in control of his aircraft.
Undaunted, he had chosen to fight on, even though he
had hardly any fuel to land safely. He was unable to eject,
perhaps due to the damage caused by the first volley of
bullets from the Starfighter.

Since all the pilots involved in the strike had returned
safely to the base and none of them had engaged with any
PAF aircraft, Taneja knew that it would have been no other
pilot than Devayya.

Group Captain Taneja wrote to the Chief of Air Staff,
strongly recommending that Squadron Leader Devayya's
gallantry be recognized by the award of a posthumous
Maha Vir Chakra, as the facts concerning his gallantry and
death had only just come to light. It took the Air Force
eight more years to conduct a thorough investigation
before recommending Devayya for the award. On that
basis, Squadron Leader Tubby Devayya was posthumously
awarded the Maha Vir Chakra on 23 April 1988, twenty-
three years after his exceptional act of conspicuous

gallantry and fighting spirit well beyond the call of duty, against overwhelming odds and at the cost of his own life.

Tubby Devayya had fought magnificently against a pilot with an aircraft far superior to his in combat power and avionics. He had not only accepted the challenge of taking on the F-104 but also succeeded in destroying his opponent, knowing full well that he could never get back to base because his fuel capacity would not allow him to do so. During his aerial combat with Amjad Hussain, he successfully carried out all the manoeuvres that he had earlier worked out in his mind. Had Tubby been able to return to the base, he would not only have had the opportunity to give a blow-by-blow account of the encounter but perhaps also to work out more innovative methods of aerial combat. This, however, was not meant to be. Today, he lies in an unknown grave in a corner of a farmer's field in Pakistan, having given his all for his country.

It was fortunate that retired Royal Air Force pilot John Fricker, while researching the history of the Pakistani Air Force, came across the narrative of the Pakistani pilot shot down by Tubby and was able to piece together a credible account of the incident; otherwise, no one would have known what had actually happened.

Notwithstanding the differences in the accounts of this air battle by the Indian and Pakistani Air Forces, the account by the PAF concludes by paying tribute to both pilots. It states, 'For many decades, this famous dogfight has confounded historians and air enthusiasts alike.' The respective Air Forces cited both pilots for courage as well as their shooting skills. Flight Lieutenant Amjad Hussain was awarded the *Sitara-i-Jurat* soon after the war. Squadron Leader Devayya was posthumously awarded the Maha Vir Chakra in April 1988, after a passage of twenty-three years. Despite the time lag of Devayya's citation, it can be said that the gallantry awards are testimony to the dogged determination of two air knights who gave their best for their own countries in this truly classic duel.

Postscript

One of the least publicized yet most creditable achievements of the 1965 air war with Pakistan was the shooting down in aerial combat of a supersonic PAF Mach 2-104 Starfighter by a subsonic IAF Mystere IVA, piloted by Squadron Leader A.B. 'Tubby' Devayya.

Sometimes, the acts of the 'Unknown Soldier' do get recognized, even though, as in this case, recognition came more than two decades after the event, and that too, due to an account by a combatant from the other side. Such events will hopefully ensure that it is never too late to recognize gallantry in war.

This story is also a tribute to Wing Commander O.P. Taneja, who persisted in fighting the bureaucratic system for eight long years to ensure justice for his colleague who gave his all for his country.

Amjad Hussain, who shot down Tubby Devayya, was himself reportedly shot down thrice and survived: first by Tubby in the 1965 Indo–Pak War and once again over Amritsar during the 1971 Indo–Pak War, where he was taken prisoner. In between, he was reportedly shot down while participating in the Arab–Israel War of 1967 but survived. If true, this could be a record of sorts.

Future Tense

There are some things that are beyond human understanding

Kanian was tall, tough, dark and handsome. At the Indian Military Academy, he was nicknamed 'Ebony' because the colour and strength of the dark hardwood best described him. His rough exterior, however, hid the fact that he was very kind-hearted and went out of his way to help anyone in need. He was also very fit and had represented the services in basketball and water polo as a young officer. Kanian, eventually, came to be well-known throughout the Army. However, the reasons for his fame had nothing to do with his professional competence, his sporting prowess or his good nature. It was actually something else!

One day, while on leave in his village, he went for a walk by the side of a river. He was familiar with the river because he and his friends had learnt to swim in it as children. While on his walk, he noticed an old man trying to cross a shallow part of the river. The elderly man suddenly stumbled and fell, and was unable to get up. The current soon carried him to a deeper part of the river, and he couldn't keep his head above the swirling water. Kanian could see that the old man was in serious trouble. He jumped in and pulled him out. The water was ice cold as the river was fed by streams originating in the Himalayas, and the old man was shivering violently. Kanian wrapped his jacket around the old man and carried him home.

The old man was frail and weak. Kanian and his parents nursed him back to health. In fact, it was Kanian's mother's home cooking that played a major part in his quick recovery.

The old man proved to be good company for Kanian's father. Every day, the old man and Kanian's father would have long conversations on history, mythology, metaphysics, astronomy and the effects of the heavenly bodies on human lives. Often, they would both be engrossed in animated discussion until late at night. From these discussions, it was clear that the old man was not only very learned but also a yogi who had spent many years meditating in the Himalayas. Despite the fact that he was a mystic, he posed no problems to Kanian's parents while staying with them. In fact, he was the perfect guest. Kanian's mother was very happy that her husband had someone so knowledgeable to talk with and that her cooking was appreciated by someone other than her family.

Her husband had been a professor who had taught for many years at Benares Hindu University, and there were many topics he could discuss with their new guest. The old man was able to clear many of her husband's doubts about the origins of the universe, the effects of the solar system on human lives, life after death and other topics to which he had not found answers in discussions with colleagues or from the many books in the University's libraries.

The elderly man had fully recovered after spending a week in their home and indicated that he had to move on. Kanian's family was reluctant to let him go. The old man said that he had never stayed with anyone for so long before and that he needed to return to his abode in the hills.

Before leaving, the old man asked Kanian how he could ever repay him for saving him from drowning and his parents for looking after him so well. Kanian and his parents assured the old man that they considered themselves blessed that he had stayed with them and that he was always most welcome in their home.

The old man said to Kanian, 'If you ever need my help, just call me and I will be there for you.'

Kanian replied, 'Maharaj ji, how will I know where you are, and how should I contact you?'

The old man smiled as if to say, 'Just try me.'

Kanian could not fathom how this would happen, but he let it rest. The old man blessed him and his parents and left.

Some years later, Kanian was in deep trouble. He had been posted to a unit that was very close to his home. The Commandant was not a nice man. He was not a happy person by nature and he also did not like to see anyone else happy. He slogged everyone in the unit and made them work even on Sundays and holidays. His only aim was his own self-advancement, and he had the habit of threatening everyone at the slightest pretext with a bad annual confidential report. No one liked him, and everyone was afraid of him too.

There was enough work in the unit to keep everyone busy without the Commandant making things worse by insisting on unproductive tasks that he felt would better his own promotion prospects. He would do anything to please his superiors, which only made matters worse. He was, however, a person who spent much time at the temple and was knowledgeable about the various rituals and practices required for various religious functions.

One day, an incident occurred that showed the Commandant's true colours. He discovered that an important confidential document in his charge was missing. His first reaction was to blame all and sundry for the lack of proper procedures in the safekeeping of documents. Next, he looked for someone specific to blame and he picked Kanian. He said he remembered giving it to Kanian, who had not returned it to him. The document contained security procedures to be followed in all units, and all officers were meant to read it and personally confirm that they had read and understood its contents. Every six months, the Commandant was to report to the higher headquarters that there was no security lapse in his unit and that the security procedures were known to all and being properly followed. He was also to confirm that the instructions had been read by all parties concerned and that the document was in safe custody.

This very document, whose safe custody was his responsibility, had gone missing. And he decided to shift the blame.

Kanian recalled handing it back to the Commandant and said so. The Commandant, however, refused to accept Kanian's reply. He yelled at him and asked him whether he, the Commandant, was telling a lie. He insisted that

Kanian had not returned the document to him and that unless it was immediately traced, disciplinary action would be initiated against him. The Commandant gave Kanian one week to trace the missing document.

Kanian did not know what to do. The unit was soon to be inspected by the Chief of Staff of Command Headquarters, and if the document was not recovered before his arrival, everyone would be in big trouble.

After a couple of days, not only the Commandant but other officers too began to give Kanian the cold shoulder, and he soon began to feel isolated. It appeared that they also held him responsible for the loss of the document, on account of which everyone was suffering.

The unit was located close to the confluence of the sacred Ganga and Yamuna rivers. It was also not too far from where Kanian's family lived. One evening, Kanian went for a walk on the banks of the Ganga without realizing how far he was going. The swirling waters reminded him of the old man he had saved from drowning. Kanian wondered where the old man was and whether he could help him out of the mess he had found himself in.

The sun was setting as he was about to return home. Beyond the confluence of the Ganga and the Yamuna, he could see the boats of the pilgrims who had come especially to pray and bathe at the junction of what was considered the holiest of rivers. It was a beautiful sight, with the boats silhouetted against an orange sky. Closer by, he watched the pilgrims bathing in the river and praying fervently. Some had launched lighted diyas (little clay lamps) into the water, which floated slowly down the river towards the setting sun. It made a pretty scene. He could also hear the chanting of the pilgrims and the clanging of the temple bells, and he marvelled at the faith of these devotees.

He recalled once again that before saying goodbye, the old man had told him, 'If you ever need my help, just call me, and I will be there for you.' Kanian wondered whether the old man meant what he said and where he was likely to be residing at the time. 'Probably in the Himalayas,' he said to himself. However, if there was a time when he really needed help, it was right then.

Kanian and his staff had assiduously and repeatedly searched every box, cupboard and shelf in their offices, but the missing file could not be traced. Kanian's suggestion that he and his staff could, with the Commandant's permission, search the Commandant's office as well was met with outrage and an angry rebuff. The Commandant shouted, 'Not only have you lost the document but you are now trying to blame me for it. Now, get lost and find the document, or I will fix you.'

If the old man had meant what he said, then perhaps it was time to reach out to him. Yet, as a soldier and a rational human being, Kanian felt a little foolish calling for someone just like that and expecting him to materialize out of thin air. Still some distance away from home, he wondered if he could try calling out to the old man then. He thought he had nothing to lose if he did, and, in any case, no one else would know. He looked around to make sure no one else was around, closed his eyes, joined his hands in fervent prayer and said out loud: 'Maharaj ji, you had promised to come to my aid whenever I was in trouble. I am now in deep trouble, indeed. Please come soon. I need your help.'

Kanian then looked around to see if anyone had observed him making this invocation. He was relieved to find no one around.

There was no response of any kind. He had not expected the old man to appear like a genie out of a lamp, yet he felt slightly disappointed.

It had turned dark and as he wended his way back home, he wondered what would happen to him. The Commandant had given him an ultimatum of one week, and five days had already passed. If the missing file was not found within the next two days, he would be subjected to a court of inquiry,[1] perhaps a summary of evidence, and possibly a court martial. All for no fault of his.

Kanian had a troubled sleep that night. He dreamt of the old man, and the dream kept recurring the whole night. In his dream, the old man was part of the river Ganga, living within its waters.

'Tell me your problem,' the old man said in his dream. 'I will resolve it for you.' Each time Kanian tried to speak, he found himself unable to articulate any words. Each time this happened, he would wake up and the dream would fade away.

He woke up late the next morning due to his disturbed sleep, and the first thing his mother said to him while giving him his early morning tea was, 'Look outside the garden gate. There is someone sitting there on the steps. Why don't you call him in and give him a cup of tea?'

Kanian did as he was told and went out to call the man in. To his astonishment, he found the old man sitting there.

'You took a long time to call me,' was all the old man said.

All the years since they had last met felt like mere days.

Kanian could not get over his surprise at actually seeing the old man right in front of him. He greeted him with great joy, touched his feet and took him into the house. Kanian's parents were delighted to see the old man again and it was a joyful reunion.

The old man said to Kanian: 'It's been a few years since I was last with you. I see some change but as you know, the old saying goes: The more things appear to change, the more they remain the same. Now, tell me what troubles you.'

Kanan told him the whole story.

'Is that all?' asked the old man.

'Yes,' Kanian replied.

The old man closed his eyes and sat in deep meditation for a few minutes.

When he was done, he opened his eyes and said, 'Let us go to your office. I would like to meet your Commandant. It is he who is responsible for this situation. Let us go and meet him.'

Kanian had a scooter at the time, and the old man clambered on to the pillion. Kanian was met with the astonished stares of the soldiers in the cantonment, who found it strange to see a sadhu sitting on the pillion of a scooter with a major in uniform. They definitely did make a strange sight! Kanian was driving at a fair speed and the old man's hair was streaming behind him, giving him a strange, surreal effect.

When Kanian reached his office, his assistant informed him that the Commandant had gone to the unit mandir.

It appeared that he had decided to requisition God to trace the missing file.

The old man assured Kanian that he would handle the situation from now on and asked to be guided to the Commandant's office.

Kanian introduced the old man to the Commandant's personal assistant and left. The old man did not want Kanian to be around when he met the Commandant.

When the Commandant returned from the mandir, he was delighted to hear that there was a holy man to see him in connection with the missing file. He believed it was an immediate answer to his prayers.

The Commandant rose from his chair when the old man was ushered into his office. He welcomed him and requested him to sit down.

The old man got down to business right away. He said, 'I understand that something valuable from this unit has been lost and that you are very disturbed about it?'

The Commandant said, 'Yes, Maharaj ji, that is true, but how have you come to know about it?' The Commandant probably expected the old man to say that it was part of heavenly intervention in answer to his prayers.

The old man replied matter-of-factly, 'The entire cantonment is talking about it, Commandant Sahib. Do you really want to know where it is?'

'Yes, yes, Maharaj ji, please.'

The old man looked at the clock and noted the time. He then asked the Commandant what appeared to be some seemingly irrelevant questions.

'Where and when were you born, and at what time?'

The Commandant seemed perplexed and was about to confront the old man on his line of questioning, but when he noticed the old man's severe demeanour, he changed his mind and answered the questions.

The old man closed his eyes, seemed to go into a trance and remained with his eyes closed for around three minutes. He then asked for a pen and paper and made some quick calculations.

Once again, he asked the Commandant a few questions.

'Is it a pale blue file with some Army crest on it?'

'Yes, yes,' the Commandant replied.

'Does the file contain twenty-seven pages?'

'I don't know,' said the Commandant.

'Hmmm,' said the old man, and closed his eyes for another three to four minutes.

He then asked, 'Do the instructions state that if the document is lost or misplaced, the loss has to be reported to higher headquarters within forty-eight hours, and have you reported accordingly that the document has been lost or misplaced?'

The Commandant hesitated for a moment, then confirmed that what the old man was saying was true, but he hadn't reported the loss of the document.

The old man then asked the Commandant in a very stern voice, 'Have you been blaming someone on your staff for this loss, knowing full well that you were making a false accusation? You must tell me the truth if you want me to find the document.'

The Commandant looked around to see whether anyone else was listening. He was perspiring as he whispered, 'Yes, Maharaj ji.'

'Hmm,' said the old man, and once again went into a silent trance.

After a while, he opened his eyes and asked, 'Do you have a steel grey cupboard marked with a large white 'X', the keys to which are always with you?'

'Yes,' the Commandant confirmed, holding up a bunch of keys and pointing to the cupboard behind the old man. The old man swivelled around in his chair to look at the cupboard, then turned back to the Commandant, closed his eyes and said, 'Open the cupboard and look at the second shelf.'

The Commandant walked across to the cupboard and did as he was told. There were just a few files on that shelf, but none of them were pale blue in colour. In a corner to the left was a red cardboard binder. The old man carried on speaking with his eyes closed and facing towards his front. 'Is there a red cardboard binder bound with white tape towards the left of this shelf?' he asked.

'Yes, Maharaj ji,' said the Commandant.

'Open it and you will find the missing file,' said the old man.

The Commandant did as he was told and found the missing file staring him in the face.

The old man had, however, not quite finished. He continued speaking with his eyes closed. 'It was you who placed this file there after looking at it three weeks ago. You placed the file there exactly at five thirty-five on the evening of the twenty-second of June.' Then he asked, 'Have you found it?'

'Yes, Maharaj ji, yes,' the Commandant confirmed.

He looked most relieved, but at the same time he felt embarrassed because he realized that the old man was absolutely right. It was he who had caused the problem, but he blamed Kanian instead.

'Good,' said the old man. 'I must go now.'

'No, no,' the Commandant insisted. 'You must stay and join in the thanksgiving at the mandir now that the lost file has been found, all thanks to you.'

'No,' said the old man. 'I must be on my way. I have other work to do.'

'What can I do to repay you?' said the Commandant.

'Tell the truth to your people,' the old man said. 'The blame for the missing file should not rest on the wrong shoulders. You will have to make a public apology. The only way to atone for your behaviour is to apologize. If you don't, it will not be good for you.'

'Yes, Maharaj ji,' said the Commandant contritely.

With that, the old man walked out of the Commandant's office without so much as a backward glance.

Postscript

The story does not end here. The Commandant did not make a public apology. He did not even apologize to Kanian in private.

The old man went back to Kanian's home and told them what had happened, staying with them for a few more days. During this period, the old man passed on the secrets of accessing the past and forecasting the future to Kanian. Subsequently, this made Kanian famous throughout the Army, but it also brought with it serious problems and necessitated a third visit from the old man. But that's another story!

The Empty Chair

There are many things in heaven and on earth that we know little about

The Regimental Centre of the Garhwal Rifles is remote and isolated. The railhead is 27 miles away at Kotdwar, and from there, the road meanders from the plains and up through the hills until it reaches Lansdowne at a height of about 6000 feet above sea level. In a way, its isolation has been a blessing that has saved it from the depredations of the so-called 'development' ruining most hill stations in India.

The view from the officers' mess on a clear morning is startlingly beautiful. An enchanting vista of the snow-clad Himalayas stretches from west to east as far as the eye can see. The mountains are barely eighty miles away as the crow flies, and on a clear day, it appears as though one could trace one's fingers in the snow with an outstretched arm. This breathtaking sight includes glimpses of glorious peaks such as Nanda Devi, Nanga Parbat, Bandar Poonch and a host of other scintillating mountains.

The forests around Lansdowne abound with oak, pine, fir, deodar and birch, with an abundance of rhododendron scattered on the ground. Human habitation being scarce in these parts, it is quite common to see panthers and leopards on the roads and tracks at night. On his rounds one night, the duty officer of the week came across a panther and her cubs playing in the moonlight on the lawns of the officers' mess. The animals watched the officer with detached interest until they finally decided it was time to leave. Man and beast live in harmony with each other in this enchanting location.

It was in this magical scenario that my meeting with the 'Regimental Ghost' took place after the Indo–Pak War of 1971.

I was wounded during the war and lost a leg, and I knew that if I wanted to continue to serve in the infantry, I needed to be able to walk in all types of terrain. The plains were not a problem, but I needed to prove to myself that I could march in the hills as well. So, after my discharge from the Artificial Limb Centre at Pune, I decided to visit my regimental centre at Lansdowne to test my leg in the hills of Garhwal and was subsequently posted to the centre.

Being an officer of the regiment, I was invited to a regimental guest night at the officers' mess one evening. The Colonel of the Garhwal Regiment, a lieutenant general from Delhi, was visiting the regimental centre on their Battle Honour Day, so there were going to be other regimental officers in attendance as well.

A Colonel of the Regiment or a Colonel Commandant of a regiment is normally a senior officer and a 'father figure' for the regiment. He has an informal role in overseeing the welfare of the personnel in his regiment.

It was early December and very cold, and both the mess ante-room and the dining room had fires burning in their hearths. The officers looked very smart in their rifle green winter mess dress. The glitter of the silver on their pouch belts and their miniature medals enhanced the smartness of their uniforms.

Cocktails before dinner took place under the benign gaze of previous Commandants staring at us from their portraits on the wall. Music by the regimental brass band wafted in from the bandstand. The band played tunes that brought back memories of the old timers of time spent in distant corners of the world during World Wars I and II. I recognized 'Lily Marlene', 'The Long Road to Tipperary' and 'Johnnie Comes Marching Home', among others.

As visitors moved around the ante-room, the oil paintings on the walls informed them that the Garhwal Regiment had two soldiers awarded Victoria Crosses during World War I. The first was Darwan Singh Negi, who was honoured with the highest British gallantry award for his role in the battle of Festubert, and the other was Gabbar Singh Negi, honoured for his conduct at the battle of Neuve Chapelle. Both their portraits were on the wall.

While walking from one painting to another, I came across the portrait of a British officer. There was something eerie about the painting! Perhaps it was the way he looked at me from his place on the wall. I wondered whether it was the effect of the lighting or the artist's skill that made me feel that way. Was it my imagination or were his eyes questioning me? I noticed his captain's badges of rank, and I wondered why his painting was on the wall and what he had done to deserve this honour. I was still gazing at him when the Deputy Commandant of the centre joined me.

'Young man,' he said. 'Do you know who he is and why he is there?'

'I know who he is, Sir,' I said, 'because his name is on the silver plate below the painting, and I have heard the name, but I do not know in what connection.'

'It's strange that you don't know,' said the Deputy Commandant. 'As a regimental officer you ought to have known!'

'Well, Sir,' I replied. 'We were commissioned into the regiment in June 1971 and sent straight to our battalions with war clouds looming on the horizon. I got wounded during the war and here I am, in the regimental centre after about one year's service, with hardly any knowledge of the history of the regiment.'

'Well,' said the Deputy Commandant, 'I will have to set that right. Come to my office tomorrow and collect a copy of our regimental history. However, as far as this painting is concerned . . .' His monologue was stopped short by a bugle call signalling that it was time to move in for dinner.

It was the duty of each officer to look at the seating plan displayed in the foyer, to identify the lady placed on his right and to escort her to her seat at the dining table. The table seated approximately thirty people. I had studied the seating plan and identified the lady I was to escort. She happened to be the daughter of one of the officers of the regiment. She was pretty and attractive, and her name, according to the seating plan, was Preiti Mathur. I felt intimidated. Pretty girls had that effect on me. I was shy around girls and the attractive ones left me tongue-tied.

I noticed her searching for her escort, so I walked up to her and introduced myself.

'I was looking out for you,' she said. 'I thought maybe you hadn't come and I would have to find my way to my seat on my own.'

I apologized and mumbled something about not being very comfortable with ladies and that I found it difficult to make conversation, particularly with pretty ones. It was a left-handed compliment that often worked. It did with her too.

She laughed and said, 'Not to worry. I'm a good talker and I'm sure that we will have a lot to talk about.' Her laugh was like the sound of silver bells and she had the cutest dimples on both cheeks. Before I could notice anything else about her, she caught hold of my arm as if it were the most natural thing to do and I walked her to her seat. Because I was a junior officer and she was so young, we were placed at the farthest end of the dining table.

We all stood behind our chairs, waiting for the chief guest—the Colonel of the Regiment. Custom dictates that no one sits before the chief guest does. However, the general was answering a call from Delhi and so we all had to wait.

While waiting, I noticed a vacant chair opposite us at the end of the table. I wondered if some poor soul had lost his way and would have to go hungry that night or whether he would be able to slip in just before the chief guest took his seat. I had nightmares about situations like this and I was glad it wasn't me!

The polished mahogany dining table gleamed in the reflected light of the dining room's main chandelier, and the mess silver shone brightly, adding to the lustre of the regimental crockery, cutlery and glassware that was arrayed before us. Place cards in silver holders were kept in front of each guest. We stood there for some time until the chief guest finally arrived. He apologized for keeping us waiting and sat down, after which we were all able to sit as well, accompanied by the sound of chairs being dragged across the wooden floor.

The chair in front of us remained unoccupied!

Soup was served. On guest nights, service begins with the chief guest on one side of the table and the next most senior guest seated opposite, and the serving of food goes sequentially down the line in opposite directions. In this manner, we and those opposite us were the last to be served.

To our surprise, the empty place was served as well. Preiti and I looked at each other in surprise. She arched her eyebrows and I looked questioningly at the nearest regimental officer. He shook his head to indicate that I should not say anything.

The unspoken question and the absence of an answer, however, loomed over us, and we kept looking at the empty chair and the untouched soup.

Preiti was easy to talk to, and we found that we shared similar interests. Listening to her prattling away, I became increasingly aware of how attractive she was. Her smile was gorgeous and her brown eyes reflected an inner beauty. She used her hands expressively while talking, and I could not help but notice her finely shaped hands and manicured nails, which were neither long nor short but just right to my way of thinking and not garishly painted. She seemed to be a girl after my own heart. More of a tomboy, in fact, and so easy to get along with! With her, I had lost my shyness completely.

She was involved with Indian dance forms and believed in keeping traditions alive by organizing talent contests and dance competitions in Kathak, Bharat Natyam, Odissi and Kuchipudi for the young. Although I had no knowledge of Indian dancing, I knew she was right about preserving our indigenous culture.

The soup plates were removed and replaced with freshly warmed plates by the servers for the next course and so it went on. The empty chair continued to be served, and the plates were removed with the food on them still uneaten.

No one else paid attention to this strange service to an empty chair except Preiti and me. Perhaps the empty chair was out of view of those further away, and those who were closer must have known what it was all about.

The wine glasses were filled for toasts to be drunk. The first toast is always to the President of the Republic of India and is drunk with water. The next toast is normally to the regiment and is drunk with wine. Water and wine were filled for the empty seat as well and subsequently removed. Each time this happened, there was a break in our conversation, and we continued to wonder what the empty chair was all about.

Dinner finally came to an end. The chief guest and the host got up, followed by all of us, and there was a lot of noise once again from chairs scraping across the wooden floor. I helped Preiti move her chair, and she thought that was very courteous. She said, 'You Army guys are so chivalrous. Wish we could see more of this outside of the Service.'

Being the most junior, we were the last to leave. Preiti picked up her place card and so did I. I walked across to the empty chair and I picked up the place card of the absent guest to find out who he was. I was surprised to find out that the name on the card was none other than that of the British officer whose portrait I had been looking at earlier in the evening! I showed the card to Preiti. The mystery of the 'empty chair' had deepened.

I asked Preiti how long she would be staying at Lansdowne and was disappointed to learn that she was leaving for Delhi early the next morning and then flying off to Singapore. I wanted to write to her but felt shy about asking if I could. She probably read my thoughts and said, 'You must find out more about the empty chair and let me know.'

I said, 'I will have to write to you, but I don't have your address!' She quickly scribbled her address on her place card and handed it over to me. I did the same. It felt good to know that we could write to each other and keep in touch.

I escorted her to the foyer, where the ladies were being helped into their coats and shawls. I handed her over to her parents. Her father was a brigadier. She hadn't told me that! Her parents were warm and kind, and they thanked me for taking care of their daughter.

I saw them off to their car. After they left, I kept looking at the red tail lights of their receding car. It was strange, but

I suddenly felt lonely. I thought I had a glimpse of a hand waving out to me and that was a good memory to take away.

The next morning, after breakfast, I called for the mess havildar to find out about the 'empty chair.' He was busy winding up the arrangements of the previous night, but he said that the empty chair was meant for the 'Captain Sahib', pointing to the portrait on the wall.

That day and the next happened to be busy, in preparation for the visit of the Army Commander scheduled for the following week.

I asked a number of officers, JCOs and NCOs about the story of the 'Captain'. Each gave his own garbled version. I finally went to the library of the regimental centre, where I managed to get some semblance of the story.

It went like this: Before the commencement of World War I, the 'Captain' was the adjutant of the Garhwal Regimental Centre at Lansdowne. Like many other British officers of that period, the 'Captain' was totally dedicated to his regiment. He knew every soldier by name. He spent his annual leave visiting his men's homes in their villages in rural Garhwal, rather than going to his home in England. He spoke Garhwali fluently and was well acquainted with their customs and traditions. Most of all, he knew the difficulties that the Garhwali villagers faced in eking out their livelihoods amid the harsh environment of the foothills of the Himalayas.

As adjutant of the regimental centre, the 'Captain's' focus was the training of the guards and sentries. Nothing but the highest standards of discipline, drill and behaviour were acceptable to him.

World War I broke out in Europe on 28 July 1914. It was a war that would cause the deaths of 20 million civilians and more than 10 million armed forces personnel. It would change the world; empires would topple, monarchies would fall and political systems would get realigned worldwide. Revolutions would usher in new ideologies and social orders would shift irrevocably. The reverberations of this war would also be felt in faraway Lansdowne, when battalions of the Garhwal Regiment would be moved to fight on the battlefields of Europe.

The 1st and 2nd battalions of the Garhwal Rifles left Lansdowne on 20 and 21 August 1914 and embarked for France from Karachi on 21 September, arriving at Marseilles on 14 and 13 October, respectively. The battalions disembarked at Marseilles and were welcomed joyously by the citizens of France. After just one day of orientation, they moved to the front lines in France, right when their services were most needed to relieve a desperate situation. Among the officers shipped out to these battlefields was the 'Captain,' accompanied by his beloved Garhwali soldiers.

Both battalions were part of the Indian Corps, which reinforced the British Expeditionary Force holding the line against the Germans in the Ypres Salient. The Garhwalis held the line against the German onslaught and fought a number of fierce battles on the battlefields of France and Flanders.

On 23 November 1914, the Germans broke into the trenches being held by the Indians at Festubert. There was much hand-to-hand fighting and several trenches were lost. Orders were received that the original line had to be restored before dawn and held at all costs.

These orders were obeyed, but a fall of snow in the night made the Indians easy targets for German rifle and machine-gun fire.

Notwithstanding this, on 24 November 1914, the Indians secured the trenches that had been lost and captured over 100 German prisoners. When the battle was over, it was discovered that Darwan Singh Negi of the 1st Garhwal Rifles had continued fighting despite being twice wounded in the head. It was only when his company had lined up after the action that his Commanding Officer noticed that he was streaming with blood from head to foot. He had led the advance of his company against the German trenches, using his kukri with skill and dexterity. He was awarded the Victoria Cross—Britain's highest award for displaying valour against the enemy.

The 'Captain' was proud that his men had fought so well but was concerned at the high rate of casualties in his company. He made sure that the wounded received proper medical attention and personally ensured that they were evacuated to military hospitals in the rear. He also ensured that the dead were properly cremated and personally wrote letters to the 'next of kin' informing them how bravely their men had fought. All this took considerable time and effort in the confusion that prevails on the battlefield in war, and he had no time to catch up on his sleep.

The 1st Garhwal Rifles, as part of the Indian Corps, thereafter moved to Neuve Chapelle. On 10 March 1915, at the battle of Neuve Chapelle, British and Indian troops attacked across a 4000-yard front, crossed 'No Man's Land' in three successive waves and assaulted the enemy without the support of artillery fire. Not a man returned.

Each one of the attackers—almost a thousand—had been killed. Among them was the 'Captain'. He had led his beloved Garhwalis in a final attack, from which he too never returned.

In the autumn of 1915, the Indian Corps was withdrawn from front-line fighting in France after a year of intense combat and severe casualties. After protecting the Suez Canal for a while, the Garhwalis returned to Lansdowne for reorganization and refit before returning to active combat.

It was around this time that the Regimental Ghost started making his appearance. The first time this happened was after a guest night at the officers' mess. The duty officer of the week had yet to check the guards by night, and he decided to use the opportunity of a late night at the mess to check the guards after dinner. Around midnight, accompanied by an orderly with a hurricane lantern, he set off on his trek to the quarter guard about a mile away from the mess. There was a strong, cold wind howling through the pine trees that night, and the orderly was doing his best to ensure the light in his lantern did not go off. However, it was a losing battle, and the light got snuffed out when they were just short of the quarter guard.

The inspection of the quarter guard by the duty officer involves a procedure where the sentry, on seeing the duty officer, challenges him by shouting *'Tham; kaun ja raha hai?* (Halt! Who goes there?)' On receiving the answer 'Grand Rounds', the sentry alerts the guard, which turns out for inspection.

On this particular occasion, when the duty officer arrived in the vicinity of the quarter guard, he noticed that something extraordinary was happening. First, the guard had already been turned out! Next, he noticed the men whispering among themselves, which went against all norms of military discipline. Then, the Guard Commander and his deputy were peering over a small stone wall, below which there was a sheer drop of about sixty feet. Finally, and most importantly, the guard had not noticed his arrival and no challenge was given.

The duty officer called out to the Guard Commander and sternly rebuked him. Discipline reasserted itself. The challenge was given by the sentry and answered by the duty officer, and the guard was inspected according to laid-down procedure.

After the guard was dismissed, the duty officer demanded an explanation from the Guard Commander for the inexplicable behaviour of the guard.

The latter reported that, about ten minutes before the arrival of the duty officer, the sentry had seen and challenged an officer mounted on a white horse. On being challenged by the sentry, the officer, in accordance with the laid-down procedure, replied, 'Grand Rounds'. The officer then proceeded to inspect the guard after it was turned out, without dismounting from his horse. After inspecting the guard, the officer turned his horse towards the low wall guarding the drop beyond the quarter guard and leapt clean over the wall, disappearing without a sound into the depths below. When the duty officer appeared, the Guard

Commander and his deputy were completely shaken and peering over the wall.

'Did you recognize the officer?' asked the duty officer, to which the Guard Commander replied that it was a British officer who had spoken in Garhwali when inspecting the guard.

The duty officer searched all around and went down the hill below the stone wall to look for any indicators to support the reported incident, but there were no hoof marks or anything else to corroborate the Guard Commander's story. He returned to his quarters baffled over what the guard had actually seen. The duty officer ordered the Guard Commander to report to the adjutant's office at orderly room the next day, along with the guard.

The next day, at orderly room, the Guard Commander and the guard were lined up to give an explanation for their behaviour the previous night. The Guard Commander stuck to his story, which was corroborated by every member of the guard.

The adjutant sent for an album from the officers' mess and the Guard Commander was taken aside and shown an officers' group photograph. Without a moment's hesitation, he pointed out the officer who had turned out the guard the previous night.

It was the 'Captain!'

As expected, the story spread like wildfire among the men, and it was not long before further incidents occurred. The next visit by the 'Captain' was reported to the adjutant a week later. This time, the officer on the white horse inspected the guard meticulously and, speaking in a 'hollow voice', instructed the Guard Commander to report Rifleman Shib Singh for having a button undone on his tunic. After his inspection, the officer vanished once again by jumping his horse over the wall.

Thereafter, incident followed incident. Strangely, each incident preceded the inspection at night by the regular duty officer of the week, who invariably would find the guard already fallen in and already inspected by the 'Captain'. It also became common for the Guard Commander of the preceding night's guard to report the next day to the adjutant minor faults of the members of the guard, such as poor turnout, unpolished leather or clumsy arms drill, which had been pointed out by the 'Captain'.

The standard of turnout and drill of the regimental guards improved perceptibly under the strict supervision of the 'Captain'. Soldiers from the hill tribes of India are notoriously superstitious; however, after a while, fear turned to pride, and it became a matter of honour to be inspected by the Regimental Ghost. However, not once did an officer set eyes on the 'Captain'.

After a year at Lansdowne, battalions of the Royal Garhwal Rifles moved again on active service, this time to Mesopotamia. With their departure, the visits by the Regimental Ghost ceased, probably because the lines were temporarily taken over by a unit of another regiment.

At the end of the war in 1918, the Garhwalis returned to Lansdowne and reoccupied its barracks. Almost immediately, the 'Captain' recommenced his inspection of the guards at night.

One night, during a particularly violent thunderstorm, the cantonment was wrapped up in mist and visibility was restricted to less than fifty yards. Thunder reverberated in the valley and flashes of lightning illuminated a ghostly scenario. A young recruit was on duty at the magazine guard responsible for the arms and ammunition of the centre. Burdened with this important duty and overawed by the scary elements of the storm, he peered continuously through the mist that swirled around his area of responsibility. Then, to his horror, he saw what appeared to be a man riding a white horse. He raised his rifle and challenged. There was no reply of 'Grand Rounds' as was expected of anyone coming to inspect the guard. He challenged again and yet there was no reply. The intruder continued his inexorable advance towards his sentry post. Alone and terrified, the young sentry fired, and the sound of his shot reverberated across the valley. The ghostly figure on the white horse disappeared, and the mist closed in on the eerie scene. The Guard Commander who had heard the shot came at the double to find out what had happened. The young sentry briefed the Guard Commander as to what had occurred.

The young sentry was marched up the next day to the adjutant and was reprimanded for the unwarranted firing of government ammunition at a ghost. He had to pay a fine of one rupee to cover the cost of the unauthorized use of government ammunition, and there the matter rested. However, after that, the frequency of inspections of the guards and sentries reduced. Sightings of the 'Captain' were now restricted to full moon nights on the roads and tracks of the Centre.

I sent Preiti a letter about the findings of my research on the Regimental Ghost and his connection with the 'empty chair'. Within a few weeks, I received her reply. She wrote:

Dear Surinder,

Thank you for your letter and for all the information regarding the 'empty chair' and the 'Regimental Ghost.' I find all this very interesting.

Now, let me now tell you about developments on this side.

Last week, I attended a function at a community hall in Singapore. Strangely, the first two rows were kept vacant! On asking why, I was told that they were reserved for 'friendly ghosts'! What a coincidence, I thought—many empty chairs! Apparently, this is a Chinese custom and is being followed in Singapore due to a large Chinese community in this country.

This letter is being sent to you care of the Regimental Centre because I know that you are still there.

I am also looking at the subject of 'friendly ghosts' in China and Japan. Will get back to you after I get the requisite information.

Do let me know if you have any more interesting facts about the 'Regimental Ghost'. I am finding the story very fascinating.

Warm regards, and best wishes for your further investigations.

Warmly
Preiti

I was happy to be able to exchange letters with Preiti. It was the Regimental Ghost that had given us this opportunity to communicate with each other and I was grateful.

Meanwhile, I discovered that, on the regimental guest night attended by Preiti and myself, the Regimental Ghost was sighted by a group of soldiers returning from the range after night firing. The sighting seemed to be part of a pattern followed by the Regimental Ghost, because I recalled reading that the first time the Regimental Ghost was sighted also happened to be after a regimental guest night!

The next regimental guest night was due to take place during the visit of the Army Commander, which was fixed for Wednesday, 20 December 1972. On that night, the moon would be in its fourth quarter. I recalled that the first time the Regimental Ghost had made its appearance, it was also a Wednesday, and that that particular night happened to be a regimental guest night. It seemed to me that there was a connection between regimental guest nights, the empty chair, the full moon and the appearance of the Regimental Ghost! I decided that the coming regimental guest night was the ideal night to catch up with the Regimental Ghost. I shared my thoughts with the mess havildar.

The mess havildar said that he felt the story was fabricated by over-imaginative soldiers who were also superstitious and confused, and that serving food to an empty chair was a waste of time, effort and food. The food had to be thrown away because no one was prepared to eat food that was meant for a ghost, regimental or otherwise. He said that the custom of the empty chair for the 'Captain' had been initiated on the advice of an officer many years earlier. The reasoning was that, since the 'Captain' conducted his nocturnal visits normally after a guest night, it would perhaps be appropriate that, since he was around, arrangements be made to invite him and keep a place for him at the dining table of the officers' mess. The mess havildar also stated that he was prepared to accompany me after the guest night, but that I should inform the adjutant that I would be taking a midnight walk after the next guest night so that the guards and sentries were warned and aware that a Regimental Officer would be walking around the centre that night and not to confuse him with the Regimental Ghost.

I wrote another letter to Preiti:

Dear Preiti,

Thank you for your letter telling me about the 'friendly ghosts' of Singapore.

Yes, it is quite a strange coincidence—this business about the 'empty chairs' in Singapore.

As mentioned in my last letter to you, the first appearance of the Regimental Ghost took place on a Wednesday after a regimental guest night. Also, there was a reported sighting of the Regimental Ghost on the guest night that we both attended, which happened to be a Wednesday when the moon was full.

There will be another guest night on Wednesday, 20 December, which also happens to be a full moon night. I have decided to take a walk around the cantonment after the guest night to see if there is any truth in these stories. Most probably, nothing will happen, but if anything is to happen, this night would be the ideal night, and I don't want to have regrets later on that I did not investigate. The mess havildar has volunteered to accompany me. I have had to inform the adjutant, and he has directed that I should take an NCO with me, so the mess havildar is welcome.

Looking forward to your research on the friendly ghosts of China and Japan. Wish you were here.

With warm regards,
Surinder

I spent the early part of that night writing this letter to Preiti, bringing her up to date on what had happened so far. An officer was leaving for Delhi the next day, and I requested that he post my letter to Preiti at the Vasant Vihar P.O., which had a special box for foreign mail. There were still five days left for the next guest night on the occasion of the Army Commander's visit.

The next few days were spent making inquiries as to the roads and tracks most frequented by the 'Captain', and a coherent pattern began to emerge. I made my plan accordingly.

The mess havildar confirmed that he would be getting the password for that night to allow us to move safely through the lines.

The guest night took place as scheduled. Fortunately, there were not too many ladies, and so I did not have to escort anyone to their seat. Though I did miss Preiti's presence. It would have been nice if she was also at Lansdowne.

The moon was out on those nights and that made me miss Preiti all the more. I wondered whether there was any connection between the moon and the feelings of men and women for each other. 'Yes,' I thought to myself, 'the moon may have something to do with it.' The lyrics of the song 'Magic Moon', which had been a hit a few years earlier, kept haunting me and running constantly through my mind. After a while, the song became synonymous with my recollections of Preiti, and I just couldn't get her off my mind.

The guest night finished early, as the Army Commander desired to have an early night, and so we were able to leave for our walk well before midnight. The moon was playing hide-and-seek behind slowly moving clouds, creating a pattern of light and shade. Rustles in the bushes sent us messages that there were animals on the prowl, and at one bend in the road, there was a low-throated growl from a bush. Light from a torch revealed a panther crouched over a kill.

We left it alone and carried on walking for a while when the mess havildar suddenly caught hold of my arm and said, 'Sahib, there's someone coming down the track.' We stood still, and yes, I could hear some sounds, but could not define what they were. We were on a gravel track, and so the sound was muffled, but after a while, I could hear the definite sound of hoofbeats on the track.

We looked up the road. Through moonlight and shadow, and between the branches and brambles that obscured our view, we caught fleeting glimpses of a horse and rider coming down the gravel track. Suddenly, the horse and rider hove into view. The horse was white! The rider wore breeches, knee-length riding boots and an officer's winter uniform of a bygone era—similar to what one saw in our regimental mess albums. The mess havildar gripped my arm tight. His eyes were wide open. He was terrified!

The apparition was very real. Not only could we see the horse and rider, but we could also smell the horse! Military horses have a peculiar smell due to their daily grooming, and this smell is well known to those of us who have ridden bareback at the National Defence Academy and the Indian Military Academy. We could also hear the creak of the saddlery as horse and rider passed by at a trot.

The rider looked down at me, and he had the same face as the portrait of the 'Captain' at the officers' mess! He stared at me long and hard, as if to say, 'I hope you now believe that I do exist!' My hair was standing on end and the mess havildar was in a sweat. We both realized that what we were staring at and what was staring back at us was, in fact, the Regimental Ghost. The horse and rider did not stop. The horse broke into a canter and then into a gallop, and as they rounded a bend, both horse and rider sailed across a small valley. They could be clearly seen etched against the background of the setting moon. The horse's tail was streaming back and the rider was crouched close to the horse's neck, as if he were urging it over a jump. We were completely speechless until they faded out of our sight.

The mess havildar and I returned to the officers' mess. I felt I needed a whisky to get over this extraordinary experience. A sleepy *abdar* (wine waiter) was woken up, and the mess havildar told him of what we had seen. The next morning, the mess staff heard the story and it soon spread around the centre. By noon, the Commandant learnt of what had happened, and I was summoned to his office.

Outside the adjutant's office, the Guard Commanders of the quarter guard and the outlying picquets were lined up. They had all been questioned. No one had seen anything extraordinary except the mess havildar and me. The Guard Commanders were broken off, and I was called into the Commandant's office. I was not asked to sit down. The adjutant and I were kept standing.

The Commandant was obviously not pleased. He said, 'I have just heard about what apparently happened last night. I do not know what you have seen or how much whisky you drank last night. Now, enough of these ghost stories! Such stories disturb the peace and tranquillity at the Centre. I don't want to hear any more of this nonsense. Is that clear?'

'Yes, Sir,' I mumbled.

Addressing the adjutant, he said, 'Tell the mess havildar to proceed on a month's leave, so that he cools off and stops babbling about what he thinks he saw last night.'

'And as for you,' he said, looking at me again, 'no more walks and no more talks. Is that understood?

'Yes, Sir,' I said.

'Now beat it,' said the Commandant.

The adjutant and I quickly exited the Commandant's office before he had anything more to say. It appeared that the Commandant was sensitive about the Regimental Ghost. I understood his sensitivity, but I could not rationalize logic with what the mess havildar and I had witnessed the previous night.

I never did believe in ghosts until the night of 20 December 1972, when I came face to face with the Regimental Ghost at Lansdowne. However, now I do believe that such things can happen and that these occurrences are beyond our understanding.

I also do believe that after guest nights at the Garhwal Regimental Centre at Lansdowne, particularly if it happens to be a Wednesday and a full moon night, the 'Captain' does go around the regimental centre of his beloved Garhwali soldiers, checking if all is well.

Postscript

I wrote to Preiti, telling her all that had happened, and a lively correspondence followed. I subsequently visited Singapore, ostensibly to learn more about the friendly ghosts of China and Japan, but really to get to know Preiti better. These visits multiplied and our friendship slowly grew into a close relationship, and we finally got married in December 1975. We owe our marriage to the Regimental Ghost, and I am sure you would have guessed by now that we spent part of our honeymoon at Lansdowne. Yes, there was an 'empty chair' at the wedding ceremony, kept in honour of the 'Captain' who had been instrumental in bringing us together.

The Sign of the Cross

*No person has ever been rewarded for what
he has 'received'
He is always rewarded for what he has 'given'
to others*

It was Padma's first fancy dress party. Major Pillay, his father, had just arrived in Bangalore from Naga Hills. It was December 1979 and this was his first leave. He had brought with him a Naga spear, a Naga dah[1] and a Naga shawl from the Zeliarong tribe. One of the pastors had gifted Major Pillay a crucifix as a goodwill gesture for all his work towards improving life in those inaccessible villages. The crucifix was suspended on a cord, and the pastor placed it around the major's neck with a prayer and blessing from the village to protect him and his family from all harm.

Little did Major Pillay realize the part the crucifix would play in the lives of his family members many years down the line. For the moment, the shawl and spear would help in dressing Padma up as a Naga warrior for the fancy dress party.

8 December 1979

The fancy dress event was part of the Army Supply Corps Raising Day celebrations, and the Centre officers' mess was decked up for the occasion. Padma's parents hoped their son would receive a prize for his out-of-the-ordinary costume. However, until then, Padma hadn't even seen a Naga warrior, witnessed a tribal war dance or heard their war cries. His father tried to make up for this deficiency by coaching him to do a reasonable imitation of a Naga war dance. Mrs Pillay and the servants could scarcely conceal their laughter as they watched father and son prancing around on the lawn of their house while making strange, loud sounds.

At the time, Padma was just twelve-and-a-half years old. When it was his turn to go up on stage, he jumped around in what he thought was a Naga war dance, and just at the crucial moment when he had to shout his war cry, his voice broke. Instead of a full-throated war cry, all he could manage was a pre-teen croak. Greatly surprised and deeply embarrassed, he tried to make up with a more vigorous jump that, unfortunately, dislodged the shawl draped around his shoulders; so he ended up looking quite strange jumping around in his vest and shorts. The audience howled with laughter, and when the winners were announced, Padma was awarded a consolation prize for the most entertaining costume and performance. It was not what Major Pillay had hoped for, but fortunately, he had a sense of humour and laughed it off.

However, Padma was deeply unhappy with his performance, and he decided right then that he would do something worthwhile and meaningful with his life and make the world sit up and take notice of him and not treat him as an object of humour.

Soon after completing his education at the Bangalore Military School, he joined the National Defence Academy and later the Indian Military Academy, and was commissioned into the 4th Battalion of the Brigade of the Guards (4 Guards), an old unit with an outstanding reputation for gallantry and chivalry in war. After five years with 4 Guards, Padma volunteered for a posting to the north-east.

In 1993, when leaving to join 8 Guards, his new unit in Manipur, Major Pillay handed over the crucifix to Padma and told him that he should temper military force with a benign policy to befriend the Naga tribes, as they were misguided by troublemakers to take the law into their own hands; that they were basically good people and needed the hand of friendship, welfare and development.

At the time, Manipur was in a state of unrest. There was an ongoing tribal conflict between the Kuki and Naga tribes and the Manipuris, and a state of insurgency had been declared. Wanton killings and unlawful action between these groups increased to the extent that the state government had to request the Army to intervene, and military operations began to rein in the ongoing terror and violence.

19 January 1994

On 19 January 1994, the battalion received information about a group of militants holed up in a village close to Longdipabran, a village within the battalion's area of operations. Captain Padma Pillay was tasked with conducting a raid to get hold of these militants and handing them over to the law-enforcement agencies, i.e., the police. Padma had just about five years' service at that time. His Commanding Officer felt that it was time for Padma to conduct a military operation independently, and so he was selected for the task.

Padma was in the officers' mess that evening when he received the orders. He quickly apprised himself of his task, the information regarding the militants and the details of the village. Having done that, he summoned the patrol that he was to lead and briefed them on the likely scenario and how the raid would be conducted.

Before leaving for his task, he remembered his father's words of advice when operating against insurgents. Just as he was getting out of his *basha*,[2] his eyes fell on the crucifix that was hanging on the wall above the door. He also recalled the words of the pastor, that the crucifix would protect his father and his family. On the spur of the moment, he took the crucifix off the wall, put the cord around his neck and tucked it under his shirt.

Within the hour, he and the soldiers of his platoon had drawn their weapons from the Company *kote*[3] and left for the village. It was a dark night, but the stars were out and the visibility was fairly good. The vehicles moved without lights, and when they reached some distance from the village, Padma decided to go on foot. Sound carries far at night in isolated areas and the noise of the vehicles would have alerted the village sentries, thereby hampering the surprise element needed for their task.

Padma had been given a guide who knew the various paths to the village. He told the guide to take them on a track that was rarely used. The guide said that he knew of such a route but had never used it. Padma decided to take the risk of going on this track, although it was not familiar to the guide.

This track approached the village from the rear. Soon, they were moving on a jungle track. It was completely dark, as the light shed by the stars was filtered out by the thick foliage.

Padma ordered the men to close up so that no one would lose contact with the man in front of him, and they moved silently in the dark. On the way, they heard jackals calling, and they wondered whether these were real animal sounds or Naga sentries passing messages that some movement was afoot and that there was danger lurking in the dark.

Finally, they emerged out of the jungle. The hillock on which the village was located was clearly visible in the light of the stars. Right at the top of the hill, they could see the outline of the village church.

The path had taken them behind the village, and they began the climb without making any noise. Naga villagers do not keep dogs as pets, so on that count they were safe, as dogs usually give early warning of strangers approaching.

When they reached the village, they noticed someone suddenly run away. It was obvious that their movement had been detected, and the man was going to warn the insurgents that the military was upon them. Fortunately, the man ran right into the arms of the men of Padma's second section, who were moving forward from the left. It turned out to be a boy who was doing sentry duty. He was quickly gagged so that he could not deliver his warning.

Padma now had the village church in front of him. He decided to check whether it was being used by the insurgents as a hideout, but it was empty except for a solitary lamp burning in a corner. The lamp shone on the figure of Jesus Christ crucified on a cross. This cross once again reminded Padma of the words of the pastor.

Padma put his hand into his shirt and felt reassured that the cross was close to his chest. He said a quick prayer to the figure on the cross, 'Jesus, I have come here on a mission to apprehend some militants. These are Indian citizens and also your children. Please help me to do my job in the best interests of my country and of these people.'

Padma then walked out of the church. He had deployed his sections around the church and sent scouts to find out where the insurgents were hiding. The scouts zeroed in on a hut, from which some light was emanating and some conversation could be heard. The guide confirmed that this would be the hut that the militants were operating out of.

The soldiers looked at Padma for directions on what he wanted them to do. Padma knew that if there was danger, as an officer, he needed to lead his men from the front. He loaded his Sten machine carbine, not realizing that the 'click' of the weapon being loaded would warn the militants of danger in the air. Immediately, there was movement within the hut, with people whispering to one another.

Padma realized that the surprise element had been lost. He kicked the door open and saw a militant aiming his weapon at him. Padma and the militant fired together at the same time. Both bullets found their targets. Despite being wounded, the militant let off another burst from his weapon, which caught Padma on the arm, with one bullet hitting him on the chest; yet, Padma didn't fall. A grenade had also been thrown by another militant, which, fortunately, did not do too much damage because the door fell and protected Padma. However, some splinters injured his leg.

Now that the surprise had been lost, both sides opened fire. In the process, one militant was killed, some were wounded and a haystack caught fire, illuminating the whole scene. A few militants tried to escape, but there was enough light to see their movements, and all of them were caught.

Of the two bullets from the militant's weapon that were aimed at Padma's chest, one caught him in the arm, but the second bullet that got him on the chest would have gone straight to his heart.

However, Padma was safe because it was the cross that took the bullet. One arm of the cross was broken. It was this arm of the metallic cross that had saved Padma's life by deflecting the bullet away from his heart. However, he had lost a lot of blood from his other wounds and needed immediate attention. A radio message requesting help was broadcast, and at first light, a helicopter descended on an open space near the church.

Unfortunately, two young village children—a seven-year-old boy and a girl aged thirteen—were wounded in the crossfire and were also in need of immediate medical attention.

The helicopter had only been authorized for the evacuation of wounded military personnel and not civilians. Padma refused to be evacuated unless the children were evacuated too, but the chopper could accommodate only two people.

An argument ensued. The pilots were in a quandary. They had been tasked to evacuate an Army officer injured in a military operation, but the officer concerned was refusing evacuation and insisting that two Naga children be evacuated first. Padma then expressed that it was his final wish.

That settled it. The two children—Dingamang, the seven-year-old boy, and Masebiliu, the thirteen-year-old girl—were evacuated first and safely delivered to the battalion headquarters at Tamenglong and then to the nearest military hospital. The helicopter then returned for Padma. Thereafter, the battalion took charge and made all the arrangements for the treatment and care of the children.

Far away in Longdipabran, the villagers were amazed at the selflessness of the young Army officer who put the safety of two young Naga children before his own. They immediately held a prayer service for the speedy recovery of the children, Dingamang and Masebiliu, and for Padma, the Indian soldier.

After the operation was wound up, a tally was taken of the outcome. One militant had been killed in the firefight, one had been wounded and three had surrendered. Several weapons, ammunition and other equipment were recovered.

However, the most important outcome of this operation was a change in the villagers' attitudes. They immediately made the decision to no longer support militancy and to co-operate with the state rather than get into a confrontation with it—all because of the humane and caring attitude of a young Army officer who believed in the values of the Indian Army and lived those values, even when he was badly wounded.

Captain Padma Pillay was recommended for a gallantry award, and on 26 January 1996, he was awarded the Shaurya Chakra for gallantry in the conduct of counter-insurgency operations.

Padma went on with his life in the Service, but he always wondered what happened to the two children and the man who had tried to kill him. He also wondered whether the village prospered or became a target of the militants because of its decision to no longer support militancy. He often thought of the church on the hill and of the crucifix that had saved his life.

Many years later, after the incident, while he was on tenure with the PMO at the National Security Council, Ministry of Home Affairs, Padma was asked to visit Manipur for official work. He asked for and readily obtained permission from the commander of a brigade in the Manipur Sector to visit the village of Longdipabran, where this operation had taken place all those years earlier.

8 March 2010

Word reached the village that the young officer who had conducted himself so well all those years ago and was now a colonel in the Indian Army would be visiting them. A grand welcome was accorded to Colonel Padma Pillay. The two young children who had been injured during the raid were grown up now and waited impatiently, along with their parents, to thank Padma once again for saving their lives. The village had also prospered by co-operating with the state. Standing at the back of the welcome party was the ex-militant Kainebon, who had thrown the grenade at Padma. He wondered what Padma's reaction would be upon meeting the militant who had tried to kill him.

Padma landed by helicopter at the same site from where he and the two children had been evacuated sixteen years earlier.

The pastor of the church was the first to meet Padma, then the village headman, the two young children he had saved and their parents, and then he came face-to-face with Kainebon. When Padma saw Kainebon, his mind flashed back to the night of the raid. He remembered the faces of the two militants being twisted with rage as they attacked Padma and his men. But that was a long time ago. Things had changed. The village had stopped supporting the militants, and Kainebon had learnt his lesson.

Kainebon, who was short in stature, looked up at Padma, wondering what he would say or do. Kainebon had aged considerably; his brow was furrowed; he had greyed; and when he looked up at Padma, his eyes were squinting in the sunlight. He stretched out his hand, hoping that Padma would take it.

There was a moment of pin-drop silence in the crowd. Everyone wondered what Colonel Padma Pillay would do. One way or another, Padma's response would have far-reaching effects in and beyond the village. Padma felt humbled by the gesture and realized the significance of the moment. He remembered the teachings of Jesus Christ, the man on the cross—to forgive those who do you harm.

He knew that these people also worshipped Jesus, the Son of God.

Padma grasped Kainebon's outstretched hand and pulled him in for a warm, tight hug. It was a gesture that signified that all was forgiven and forgotten. There was a perceptible gasp of approval from the crowd, followed by a lot of clapping and cheering. Tears streamed down Kainebon's face and Padma was taken aback by the intensity of the moment.

What followed was a grand welcome ceremony by the village for Padma. A hundred acres of land were given to honour him, and he was invited to build a home there and become a part of their tribe. As is the custom of the tribe, as part of the welcome ceremony, he was presented with a shawl woven by the women of the village. The tribal design and colours were a replica of the ones on the shawl gifted to his father years ago by members of the same tribe! This was a remarkable coincidence. It meant that both Padma and his father had worked for the same people, although at a different place, in a different way and at a different time! The association of father and son with these people had come full circle.

Padma was taken to the village church that he had visited so many years ago. The large cross with the statue of Christ nailed to it was still in the corner of the church, and the lamp still burned at its foot. Padma was reminded of the crucifix that had saved his life. He wondered if it was a mere coincidence or if the hand of God had actually intervened to save his life sixteen years earlier and set up a chain of events for both Padma and the village of Longdipabran.

Postscript

Padma did not accept the gift of the land, saying he wanted a place in their hearts instead, and said that he would always be part of the village family. He approached Mr Gadkari, the Minister of Roads and Surface Transport, to build a road to the village, which was accepted and work on its construction has since commenced. When completed, this road will offer access to the sale of the produce of the villagers, mainly orange cultivation, and will contribute to the development of the village in many different ways. Padma also arranged for twenty-five girls from the village to be trained as nurses at Dr Devi Shetty's hospital in Bangalore. Dr Shetty was Mother Theresa's personal physician.

Padma believes that it was really the hand of God that protected him that night. He has preserved the crucifix, one arm of which was broken off by the bullet that had been aimed at his heart.

Padma's conduct during the operation and sixteen years later, when he visited the village, confirm that winning the hearts and minds of insurgents is more important than the use of force.

Matter of Honour

Honour lost, all lost

The Rajputs are a race for whom honour matters above all else. This is also true of the Indian Army. Honour is the lifeblood of the Army's ethos and culture. Once a soldier gives his word, nothing more is needed. Contracts, written agreements and memoranda of understanding are superfluous.

The term 'gentleman cadet', by which all cadets at the Indian Military Academy are called, predisposes him to the virtues of honour, chivalry, truthfulness, duty and discipline. However, honour is above all else because the Army believes that everything flows from this all-encompassing value.

The Chetwode motto handed down to all gentlemen cadets at the Indian Military Academy epitomizes the philosophy of the Indian Army and emphasizes the importance of honour:

> The safety, honour, and welfare of your country come first always and every time.
> The honour and welfare of the men you command come next.
> Your own ease, comfort, and welfare come last, always and every time.

Soldiers of the Indian Army who are brought up with this philosophy find it difficult to adjust to the present world, where greed and self-interest are prevalent.

This is the story of a battalion of the Rajput Regiment. The narrative finds mention in Philip Mason's book, *A Matter of Honour: An Account of the Indian Army, Its Officers and Men.*

For thousands of years, the Rajputs have maintained their noble traditions of honour, chivalry, fearlessness, love for battle and utter disregard for their lives when it comes to defending the honour of their country, their clan and their women. During the period when the Indian social system was evolving, the Rajputs, or *Kshatriyas* as they were then called, were entrusted with protecting society from hostile invaders. Together with the Brahmins, who looked after the spiritual aspects of life, the Rajputs had a large say in public life and constituted the ruling class. The word 'Rajput' soon became synonymous with honour. A promise made by a Rajput was dearer than life itself. Rajput women stood for purity and honour. They sometimes made the supreme sacrifice by committing *jauhar*[1] (immolation by fire) when their men were killed in battle, rather than submitting to the will of an enemy. When their men left for battle, the doors of the fort were closed and only reopened if the men returned victorious. If they were defeated, the doors remained shut because there was no one to come back to.

Philip Mason, who recounts the above in his book, *A Matter of Honour*, has placed honour as the critical determinant that has shaped the Indian Army of today. In it, he has placed the values of loyalty to comrades, fidelity and courage as the most important factors that constitute honour. He says that without these virtues, an Army is nothing. The story of the 31st Bengal Native Infantry, later to be named 1 Rajput, illustrates the point. In 1805, this battalion was part of General Lake's force. Lake had won a series of battles against Maharaja Daulat Rao Scindia's forces.

Lake, however, met his match at Bharatpur. The fort at Bharatpur had a circumference of seven miles. The ramparts were made of mud and were 80 to 120 feet high. The fort was surrounded by a deep moat from which its colossal walls had been dug—a deep and wide ditch with plenty of water. Cannonballs had little effect on the fort. The projectiles merely buried themselves in its mud walls. Two major assaults by Lake were beaten back with heavy casualties.

Lake ordered a third assault. It was badly planned, and the leading troops were jammed in a narrow pass and suffered very heavy casualties. However, Indian infantry battalions carried on with the assault.

In military operations, the practice of carrying colours served as a rallying point for troops as well as to indicate the location of the Commander. The practice is thought to have originated in ancient Egypt around 5000 years ago. It was formalized in the armies of medieval Europe, as colours began getting emblazoned with the Commander's coat of arms.

As time passed and battles became more chaotic due to the amount of dust and smoke on the battlefield, soldiers needed to know where their regiment was, and colours served that purpose.

In due course, regiments were awarded battle honours that were emblazoned on their colours. Serving as a link to the regiment's past and a memorial to the fallen, colours, therefore, took on a more mystical significance. They became the heart of the regiment, into which all of its history was woven. For a Regiment to lose its colours was, and still is, a major disgrace, and the capture of an enemy's colours was seen as an achievement of great honour. This is why, whenever the colours are paraded, they are always escorted by armed guards and are paid the highest compliments by all soldiers and officers, second only to those paid to a President or a king.

Colours are consecrated. When they become too faded to be used, the old colours are laid to rest at a formal military parade and the new colours take their place. The old colours are laid up in a regimental chapel,[2] where they are preserved or sent to Chetwode Hall at the Indian Military Academy at Dehradun.

With the advent of modern weapons, technology and efficient systems of communication, colours are no longer carried into battle. Instead, they are carried in parades and reviews and displayed in formations and ceremonies in remembrance of their former presence on the battlefield.

Coming back to the story: The next day, Lake addressed the force and expressed regret that they had not lived up to its high standards. He requested volunteers for a fourth assault, and to his surprise, he found that every man in the Indian infantry battalions had volunteered.

The fourth assault took place on the same day. Men drove their bayonets into the walls of the mud fort and used the bayonet hilts to climb up. But a shower of logs and stones was rolled down on them, and so narrow was the way up, that musketry fire could be concentrated on the leaders.

As one man fell, he brought down those below him. The 31st Bengal Native Infantry, however, managed to place their colours on the summit. But it was a tiny party and they could not have survived. The officer carrying the unit's colours was also killed as he neared the summit, so their Commanding Officer (CO) asked the colour party to return.

In a short span of two hours, nearly 1000 men were either killed or wounded in this battle. The 31st Bengal Native Infantry had 180 men killed or wounded out of a strength of 400. Once again, the attack had failed.

The colours had been near the summit of the walls of the fort, and during the fierce fighting, they had been riddled with bullets and become tattered and unserviceable. The battalion had seen a number of its men on the summit of the fort and considered the order to return a slur on their honour.

The campaign was called off, and the units of the force went back to their original locations. As was the custom of the unit, a board of officers was held. It was their task to determine how the colours had got damaged, to order a replacement and to order the old colours to be laid up in a museum or a church or destroyed.

When the new colours arrived, they were placed in the unit quarter guard side-by-side with the old colours. The old colours were too badly damaged to retain them in a museum or a church, and so it was decided they would be cremated the next day. But in the morning, nothing remained of the old colours; every fragment had disappeared, and no officer could learn what had become of them. It was a mystery that was not pursued.

Twenty-one years later, in 1825–26, the Second Battle of Bharatpur took place, and a siege to the fort was launched for the second time. The 31st Native Infantry Battalion was once again part of the force that was to attack the fort. This time, however, they were in reserve and did not form part of the assaulting echelons.

The subedar major of the battalion, who was a young soldier when the fort was attacked in 1805, came up to the CO and reported that it was the wish of the men that they join the assaulting force. The CO was surprised because the soldiers of the assaulting force were the troops that would be exposed to maximum danger. However, he conveyed the wish of the men to the Force Commander. The Force Commander was happy to have a battalion volunteer for this hazardous task and gave his consent.

The battalion took its place right in the front of the assault force where the casualties would be the heaviest. This time, giant mines were used to breach the walls of the fort. The 31st Bengal Native Infantry surged through after a hard-fought battle, and the fort and town were captured. As expected, the battalion suffered heavy casualties.

After the battle, the Battalion Commander went around the site to assess for himself the number of those killed and to meet the wounded. However, he found something that he had failed to notice earlier. On every soldier's chest, was pinned what looked like a faded ribbon. Similar strips of ribbon were also tied to the mast of the new colours.

He realized what had happened to the old colours that disappeared twenty-one years earlier!

Fragments of the old colours had apparently been preserved as relics by the men who had taken part in the attack in 1805 and had been handed over from father to son, who preserved them over the years, to be brought out only when Bharatpur was to be attacked once again, so that they might redeem the honour and valour of their fathers.

Two generations of Rajput soldiers had waited patiently for twenty-one years to retrieve what they considered an affront to their honour.

The name of this gallant battalion has changed over time. When India became independent, the name of this unit was changed from the 31st Native Infantry to the 1st Rajput. Later, when the Indian Army raised the Brigade of Guards, it chose 1st Rajput to be part of it and renamed it the 4th Battalion, the Brigade of the Guards. The battalion has continued to carve a place of honour for itself in the wars that India has fought since Independence.

This story is symbolic of the value placed on honour by the Rajputs and the Indian Army. Honour, courage, duty and sacrifice are so interwoven into the fabric, culture and ethos of the Indian Army that they become inseparable and honour always claims pre-eminence.

And when the day's work is done, at far-flung corners of the country's borders, men gather around campfires and sing songs of the deeds of their forbearers who have blazed paths of glory in the name and *izzat*[3] of their regiments. The torch of tradition is passed from the past to the present, and when the chips are down, it is sometimes left to the next generation to carry the flame of regimental pride forward to light the way into an uncertain future.

Postscript

If you wish to follow up on this story, do visit 4 Guards. There, in their officers' mess, you will see a silver trophy that commemorates this event that took place nearly 200 years ago. Around the wooden base of this trophy, you will see little pieces of glass under which are placed fragments of the old colours, which serve as a reminder of what honour is all about—honour beyond fear!

Regimental Bonds

'My thoughts return to you who were my comrades,
the stubborn and indomitable peasants of Nepal. Once
more I hear the laughter with which you greeted
every hardship. Once more I see you in your bivouacs
or about your campfires, on forced marches or in
the trenches, now shivering with wet and cold, now
scorched by a pitiless and burning sun. Uncomplaining,
you endure hunger and thirst and wounds; and at last,
your unwavering lines disappear into the smoke and
wrath of battle. Bravest of the brave, most generous of
the generous . . .'

A tribute to the Gurkhas,
by R.L. Turner

It was quiet, too quiet! The eerie silence hung heavy in the air on a very hot and humid afternoon in Sri Lanka. Not a single leaf stirred. Unseen eyes watched as the Gorkha patrol moved slowly, bound by bound, along the jungle track.

Rifleman Neerbahadur Thapa, who had been detailed as the forward scout, moved ahead slowly, taking cover in the bushes and trees on the left of the track leading to the jungle. His sharp eyes scanned the area ahead of him, from left to right and from right to left, just as he had been taught during his recruit training at the regimental centre in Shillong.

There was no movement, no bird calls and even the insects were silent. This part of Sri Lanka seemed to be holding its breath in anticipation of the drama that was about to unfold.

Neerbahadur could read the jungle like a book. He knew that the absence of sound and movement spelt danger. He knew intuitively that there was a problem ahead. Gorkhas are essentially hunters, and silence is crucial when operating in the jungle, for both the hunter and the hunted. He had to be invisible to succeed, but how could he become invisible when he was required to move in an area with limited cover, and that too in enemy-held territory?

A battalion of the Madras Regiment had been encircled by the Tamil Tigers. The Gorkhas, who had just landed at Palel airfield, had been tasked to link up with the battalion before nightfall. The Tamil Tigers anticipated such a move and laid a clever ambush.

Neerbahadur's keen eyes detected a slight movement in the jungle to his right. The Tamil Tigers watched Neerbahadur indicate by hand signals to the Gorkha troops that were following that there was danger ahead.

Neerbahadur was undecided. On the one hand, he had been told to move fast so that the beleaguered battalion could be linked up before nightfall. On the other hand, he sensed there was danger ahead and that he was on exposed ground.

The Tamil Tigers had held their fire as they were looking for a bigger target. However, if their presence was discovered, they would be in danger of being cut off should the Gorkhas move a force behind them.

Neerbahadur decided that he needed to run forward towards the jungle up ahead, which offered cover. He got up from his position and started to run. The Tamil Tiger manning the heavy machine gun waited until Neerbahadur came to an open piece of ground and started firing when he ran across the open patch. The fusillade caught Neerbahadur on the run. The force of the bullets and the momentum of his run threw him up into the air, and he somersaulted and fell spreadeagled on the ground. Neerbahadur got hold of his weapon and fired back at his assailants, but being wounded and without cover, he caught the brunt of the enemy fire as more bullets pumped into his exposed body, killing him on the spot.

Neerbahadur's section responded immediately by firing a heavy fusillade at the ambush party, while the remainder of his company moved quickly from behind to cut off the enemy from the rear. The Tamil Tigers noticed the movement and commenced their withdrawal from the ambush site. The Gorkhas managed to intercept some of the escaping enemy, killing three and wounding many more. The firefight lasted another sixty minutes as the enemy endeavoured to take away their dead and wounded.

The battalion reorganized, resumed its advance, successfully completed its mission and returned to base, where Neerbahadur was cremated with full military honours.

Rifleman Neerbahadur Thapa, killed in that ambush by the Tamil Tigers, was a third-generation soldier of the battalion.

Gorkha soldiers are tough. Living in the hills makes them strong and resilient, and they are able to withstand the vicissitudes of war, climate and terrain better than most. They are cheerful in disposition, and nothing can disturb their equanimity. They are loyal to the core and fearless in battle. All these qualities place them among the best soldiers in the world, and they are much sought after. Soldiering is a natural profession for them, and the battalion has men from the same family who are fifth-generation soldiers, all of whom have served or continue to serve in the unit. Field Marshal Sam Manekshaw, who was from this regiment, once said, 'If anyone says that he is not afraid of dying, he is either a liar or a Gorkha.'

The battalion has some excellent customs and traditions. One of them is that when an officer is commissioned into the battalion, he spends his first leave in Nepal instead of going home. The young officer is normally accompanied by a soldier due to proceed on leave, who takes him to his own home and then hands him over to the next family to be visited; thereafter, the officer is handed over from one family to another, until all the families are visited and it is time for him to return to the battalion.

In this manner, the young officer gets to know the families of his men, their language, dialects, customs and traditions, culture, songs and dances, and the difficulties that they face in the mountainous areas of Nepal, where most of the travelling is done on foot. He meets the fathers, mothers, children and grandparents of his men and is thus initiated into their culture and traditions. The fathers and grandfathers tell him tales of battles fought in faraway lands, and the history of the battalion comes alive. When he returns to the battalion, he will have come to know every member of his men's families, and a strong bond is formed between the officer and the men he commands. The men's families associate so closely with the unit that family honour and the honour of the battalion become synonymous.

Another tradition that concerns this story comes from the grim arena of war. When a soldier gets killed in battle, all personnel of the unit, starting from the Commanding Officer (CO) down to the junior-most riflemen, contribute one day's salary to the bereaved family of the soldier. This money is collected and sent to the wife of the soldier, or his mother, if he is not married, so that the family has something to live on until the family pension commences.

As is the custom of the battalion, one day's salary was collected from all ranks to send to Neerbahadur's parents.

A junior commissioned officer (JCO) whose home was close to Neerbahadur's village in Nepal was given the task of conveying the condolences of the CO and all ranks of the battalion to Neerbahadur's parents and handing over the money that had been collected.

While the JCO was climbing up the steep mountainside towards Neerbahadur's house, he met some of the villagers who were also moving towards the village. Noticing that he was an outsider, they asked him who he had come to see. The JCO mentioned the name of Neerbahadur's father. They stopped and asked, 'Don't you know that Naik Raj Bahadur died eleven days ago?' The JCO was taken aback and did not even attempt to explain that the battalion was in faraway Sri Lanka and no message had reached them from distant Nepal. He realized that he now had to tell Neerbahadur's mother, who was already mourning the death of her husband, that she had lost her son as well!

Eleven days earlier was about the same time that Neerbahadur had been killed! He wondered whether father and son had died on the same day. It appeared to be so.

The JCO reached Neerbahadur's house after a difficult climb. The house, like most village houses in the hill areas of Nepal, was made of stone with a shingled roof of slate, and the doors and windows were made of wood. The walls were covered with a layer of brown clay and whitewashed. A small, neat courtyard had corn cobs and chillies drying in the sun. Also sitting in the sun was Neerbahadur's mother.

She was a good-looking woman whose weather-beaten face reflected the ravages of climate and the hard life that Nepalese women face while their husbands are away soldiering in far-off lands.

She rose from where she was seated to greet the JCO, whom she recognized from before. 'How did the Commanding Officer come to know that my husband has passed away?' she asked with surprise. 'My husband died just eleven days ago!'

'No, *mataji* (mother),' said the JCO. 'We did not know that your husband has passed away.' Then he added, 'How did he die, mataji?'

'He fell ill,' she said. 'He refused to let my son carry him to the hospital, which is a four-day trek from here. He passed away eleven days ago because he could not get medical attention in time.'

The JCO now realized that father and son had died on the same day, but he made no comment.

'So, what brings you here?' she asked, wiping away her tears. 'I thought you came because you heard that my husband has died. The *paltan*[1] (battalion) is in Sri Lanka, isn't it?'

'Yes, mataji,' said the JCO. 'The battalion is in Sri Lanka, which is very far away and across the sea. We have been fighting a war there for over a month. I have just arrived in Nepal because the Commanding Officer sahib asked me to meet you.'

Neerbahadur's mother gave the JCO a questioning look. 'Meet me?'

The JCO went on to say, 'I am very sorry, mataji, but I have to tell you that not only have you lost your husband, but you have also lost your son. Neerbahadur was killed about eleven days ago in the fighting in Sri Lanka.'

Neerbahadur's mother gazed at the JCO uncomprehendingly, looked for her stool and sat down. This was too much for her. She was barely coping with the loss of her husband when she learnt that she had also lost her firstborn, and that too around the same time as her husband.

Gorkha women are stoic. They do not wail, shout and beat their chest when given tragic news of the loss of their near and dear ones. But like anyone else, she felt the deep sorrow of a mother who loses her child. Tears rolled down her weather-beaten face. All her dreams for her elder son had been destroyed in a moment. She realized that one more pillar of strength had been taken away from her so soon and that life was now going to be that much more difficult.

They both sat silently, looking across the valley at the huge snow-covered mountains that marked Nepal's boundary with Tibet.

A dog barked from somewhere down below and a rooster crowed to register his presence. A cold wind from the north stirred the leaves of the nearby trees. Their world was otherwise silent. Nature seemed to sense the tragedy that continued to unfold in this small and distant hamlet.

Finally, wiping away her tears, she asked, 'How did my son die? Did he die like a good soldier? Did his death bring honour to the paltan and to my family?'

'Yes, *mataji*,' the JCO assured her. 'Neerbahadur did an excellent job. Thanks to his action, the battalion was able to break an ambush. It was because of him that many of our men were saved and many of the Tamil Tigers were killed and wounded. Thanks to Neerbahadur, we were successful during that day's battle. He was a great soldier, and he has brought honour to the battalion and to the regiment.'

Neerbahadur's mother let out a deep sigh and lapsed into silence again.

She was thinking of the past, when she had spoken to the JCO about how Neerbahadur had assumed the role of 'the man of the house' even when he was little, when his father was away. How he had decided to follow his father into the Army and the battalion, so that the link between the family and the battalion could remain intact.

Speaking softly, she said, 'We had only two sons, Neerbahadur and his younger brother, Narbahadur. When Neerbahadur decided to leave home and join the battalion, it was agreed that Narbahadur would stay at home to look after us and the family property.'

After a while, she added, 'I had found a good girl for Neerbahadur and had planned to get him married later this year, when he came on leave. That won't happen now. Only Narbahadur and I are left.' She lapsed into silence once more.

Just then, the sound of footsteps indicated that someone was approaching. It was the sound of Narbahadur's footsteps that they heard, and he soon came into view. He was carrying a heavy load of *dauro* (firewood) on his back and was preceded by a huge black Himalayan mastiff who bounded forward to sniff at and investigate the visitor. The dog had a solid leather collar with steel spikes to protect him against mountain leopards and other wild beasts that prowled around these lonely homesteads. Dogs were easy meat for leopards and panthers, but this big Himalayan mastiff was more than a match for those big cats. The spiked collar helped provide some protection.

Narbahadur saw the JCO, dumped the firewood at the entrance of the courtyard and came at a run to meet him. Visitors to the village were rare, and they brought news from the outside world. Neerbahadur's mother allowed the two of them to exchange greetings, and she then said to Narbahadur, 'Now go inside and prepare a cup of tea for Bhimbahadur Sahib,' for that was the JCO's name.

When Narbahadur had gone inside, Neerbahadur's mother said to Bhimbahadur, 'It is not right that the bond between my family and the battalion should break. It was my husband's dream that Neerbahadur would have a son and that our family's connection with the battalion would stay intact. Now that Neerbahadur is no more, you must take Narbahadur with you to the battalion and enlist him so that my family's link with the battalion remains unbroken.'

When Narbahadur came with the tea, she asked him to sit down and said, 'Your brother Neerbahadur is dead. He was killed in action in Sri Lanka. Bhimbahadur Sahib has come from Sri Lanka to give us this sad news.'

Narbahadur took the news of his brother's death quietly. He had not imagined that the JCO would bring home such unhappy tidings. He sat silently, trying to reconcile himself with this piece of unhappy news about the death of his elder brother and what it would portend for the future of the family.

After a while, the mother said to Narbahadur, 'I feel you should take Neerbahadur's place. You know your father's view on the continuity of the family's link with the paltan. That link must not break.'

Narbahadur had always wanted to be a soldier like his brother, his cousins and his friends. However, being an obedient son, he had reconciled himself to the role of looking after his parents and taking charge of the family homestead. Someone had to stay behind. If it had to be him, so be it.

Now, Neerbahadur's death had changed the situation. The circumstance, however, was an unhappy one. On the one hand, the First Fifth Gorkha Rifles was a very famous battalion, and here he was being given an opportunity to be part of this elite unit. On the other hand, he felt uncomfortable that this opportunity had come his way only because of the death of his brother. Most of all, what would become of his mother if he too went away? After a while, he spoke up and asked his mother, 'And what will become of you if I'm gone? Who will look after you?'

His mother answered, 'Who looked after me when your father was away and you and Neerbahadur were little boys? Don't worry, I can look after myself, and Bhalu is also here to look after me.'

Bhalu's ears perked up on hearing his name and he gave a reassuring growl, as if to say, 'Yes, don't worry, I will be around.'

After a while, it was time for Bhimbahadur to leave. He had to trek to his own home, many hours away. He would be able to meet with his family only for a few hours, spend the night with them and then return to the battalion. After all, there was a war on and he had to get back to it.

In the meantime, Narbahadur had packed a few clothes and was ready to leave with Bhimbahadur. He touched his mother's feet and sought her blessings. There were tears in his mother's eyes and his eyes were moist as well. Bhalu tried to join them too but Narbahadur's mother caught hold of him and made him sit.

Narbahadur accompanied the JCO and went down the footpath. He kept looking back at his mother, who was silhouetted against their little home until, at last, an intervening spur shut her out of his sight.

Narbahadur's mother went inside and wept. She could cry now, as there was no one to witness her anguish. She wept for her husband, her partner of many years, who had left her suddenly because she couldn't get him to a hospital in time. She wept for her first-born who had died a soldier's death in some far-off land, her hopes and dreams for his future destroyed forever. She wept at the departure of her surviving son, who had been the strength of the family these past few years. Finally, she wept for herself at the thought of the many years she would now have to spend alone.

Bhalu seemed to sense her discomfort and snuggled closer to her. She fondled his ears and stopped crying. She was a practical woman. There was work to be done. More than before! *No point in crying*, she whispered to herself.

She lit a lamp, paid obeisance to the light, as is the custom in village homes, then shut and barricaded the stout wooden door.

She didn't feel like eating—not tonight, at least.

Sleep and time would heal her sorrow. Today was just too much. Tomorrow would be another day.

Postscript

Narbahadur is doing well in the battalion. He has been promoted to havildar (sergeant). He has a son now, and the battalion waits for him to join their ranks so that the regimental bond can continue. When he joins them, he will be a fourth-generation son of the battalion.

Ultimately, it is these bonds that hold the Indian Army together, especially in tough times: bonds that only the Army know and understands.

Neerbahadur's mother is not alone now. Narbahadur's wife and son keep her company. Bhalu has gone on to his happy hunting grounds. He died in 1998. His son Bhote keeps his 'doggy' line intact with the family.

Family Tree

Soldier *Neerbahadur Thapa, 1/5 Gorkha Rifles (FF) Killed in action 21 January 1990*

Father *Naik Rajbahadur Thapa, 1/5 Gorkha Rifles (FF) Died of illness 21 January 1990*

Mother *Chandrakala, mother of Neerbahadur and wife of Naik Rajbahadur*

Grandfather *Subedar Chabilal Thapa, 1/5 Gorkha Rifles (FF)*

Brother *Havildar Narbahadur Thapa, 1/5 Gorkha Rifles (FF) Recruited October 1990*

The poem that follows is about this incident and the close relationship between regiments and their soldiers' families in general, and about this family of the 5th Gorkha Rifles, in particular.

Regimental Bonds

She waits in distant Nepal, on the border with Tibet
For her men who serve Fifth Gorkhas
And have not returned as yet

Father, son and husband have answered India's call
They serve with faith and honour
With a smile that conquers all

They have served for ancient decades, their line it must not break
Their footsteps must not falter
For their honour is at stake

Great battles are in progress, distant miles away
Are her men involved in fighting?
Are they in the roaring fray?

With boldness and with courage they charge the angry guns
In the wrath and smoke of battle
Families lose their gallant sons

The aftermath of battle dreary news conveys
That all her men have fallen
On those dismal, fateful days

Her family line lies broken; her links are all but gone
Her men, they all have fallen
Her line now stands forlorn

But wait! There's someone out there waiting
Her youngest son stands tall
The war is not abating and they hear the regiment's call

She asks him, 'Are you willing to take part in the fray?'
Though her heart is near to breaking
But the line must have its way

He answers, 'Yes.' He's eager. His eyes are all alight
He is thinking of his mother
But his heart is in the fight

Her son then soon enlisted. The line is now intact
He fights his father's battles
But she's alone, in fact

'He's the last one of my line, Lord, my only pride and joy
Will you keep him safe in battle?
He's just my little boy'

'Will he come home safe and sound, Lord?
He needs to have a wife
For the line to be unbroken
He must start another life.'

© Ian Cardozo, New Delhi,
7 August 2003

Answer to a Prayer

Ask, and it shall be given you; seek, and you shall find; knock, and it shall be opened unto you.

—Matthew 7:7, New Testament

For the general and his wife Anjali, it was the perfect holiday. Goa was at its best and everything had gone according to plan. The week spent at a holiday resort on the Vagator beach in north Goa had proved to be all that was advertised and more. The service was perfect, the weather was sublime, the food was out of this world, and after a great deal of effort, the reservations for the next leg of their journey had also come through. Nothing had been left to chance—or so they thought.

Vagator is Goa at its best. It has a beautiful beach with white-capped waves breaking on to its glistening sands and a profusion of sun-kissed palms waving gently in the sea breeze. A rocky promontory dipping gradually towards the beach is home to idyllic guest houses with whitewashed walls and red-tiled roofs. At mealtime, sun-tanned tourists are regaled with the aroma of exotic dishes emanating from kitchens replicating ancient recipes that have made Goan cuisine loved and imitated all over the world. The locals say that tigers roamed in this area a long time ago, and that is how it got its name. *Vag* in Konkani, the local language, means 'tiger'. It was now their last few moments left to enjoy the beauty of the beach, and they had planned every minute of it so as to make the most of a beautiful day.

The next leg of their journey to Pune held a lot of promise. They were going to be met by old friends at the Pune railway station at the ungodly hour of 4 a.m., and taken to their farm on the outskirts of the city. A reunion of friends who had fought in the 1971 War had been organized at the farm. One of them had not much time left to live, so it was important that the general and his wife arrive on time.

They were booked on the *Goa Express*, which would leave Vasco da Gama in south Goa that afternoon. It would be a long drive from north to south Goa and arrangements had been made for the same. An Army colonel, a close friend, had offered to drive them there. He had rung them up the previous evening to ask for details about their departure. He wanted to know the name of the train and the time scheduled for its departure from Vasco.

The general knew that the name of the train was the *Goa Express* but was not sure of the time of departure. He looked around for his reading glasses but couldn't find them. He peered at the ticket and saw that it contained a lot of information, all in figures. It gave the number of the train; there was something called the PNR number; the numbers of their berths; and their ages. The general finally spotted the time of departure at the bottom right-hand corner of the ticket. He looked at it again and found that the figures indicating the departure time from Vasco da Gama was 3.15 p.m.

The general informed the colonel that the train was scheduled to leave Vasco at 3.15 p.m. The officer repeated the time, as all officers are taught to do in the Army, and said since it was a two-hour drive, he would pick them up at 1 p.m., leaving fifteen minutes to spare for contingencies.

The general and Anjali went to the beach early the next morning for a last walk on Vagator's gleaming white sands and returned to the resort for breakfast and an hour's swim in the pool. The resort went out of its way to provide a nice farewell lunch for them. It was typically Goan and reflected the cuisine that the resort was famous for. Chicken soup was followed by sorpotel with sannas,[1] and pomfret caldeen with prawn pulao. The meal was washed down with port wine, and for dessert, there was the famous Goan sweet, bebinca.

They had just finished lunch when they received a call informing them that the colonel had arrived. The general looked at his watch and saw that it was exactly 1 p.m. They had already packed. Anjali left the room to meet the colonel and sent for a boy to carry their luggage. All that she asked the general to do was lock the room and bring the keys to the desk at reception.

For some inexplicable reason, the general decided to take another look at the ticket to check the time of departure. This time, he had his reading glasses on. He froze in horror when he realized that the time of departure was not 3.15 but 13.15! The first figure was slightly faded, so it had escaped his attention when he had looked at it without his reading glasses the previous evening.

This meant that the *Goa Express* would have already lined up at the platform at Vasco da Gama railway station, and they were still two hours away by road in Vagator. There was no way that they could possibly reach Vasco da Gama before the *Goa Express* left, even if they had a helicopter at their disposal.

Thoughts flashed in the general's mind: the great difficulty that they had had in getting the last two available berths on the *Goa Express* to Pune and the absolute impossibility of getting tickets on any train thereafter, as it was the Christmas season of 2002. Tourists were pouring into Goa for the New Year celebrations, so getting extended accommodation at Vagator was impossible. In the meantime, the room keys had already been collected to prepare the room for the next set of guests who were already waiting in the lobby. Worst of all, he had to break the news to Anjali and the colonel, who were happily chatting in the lobby, oblivious to what had occurred and the problems that loomed ahead.

The colonel had already strapped their luggage on to the carrier on top of his car, which was a Maruti 800.

'Hi Sir,' he said cheerfully to the general. 'All set?'

The general blurted out that the departure time of the *Goa Express* was not 3.15 but 13.15 and that the train would, in all probability, be leaving Vasco da Gama at that very moment.

The colonel looked at the general in disbelief and Anjali looked at him in horror. Their facial expressions seemed to say, 'This just can't be true; you must be joking!'

The colonel, however, was a man of action. He said, 'Let's not waste any more time, Sir. Just jump in; we'll try and catch that train wherever it is.'

They quickly got in. The colonel started the engine and took off with a roar that drowned out the grumbling that was emanating from the back seat. Fortunately, the colonel's wife had also come along and she was doing her best to calm troubled waters.

The colonel got through to his brother on his mobile. Their village was en route. He asked him to find out whether the *Goa Express* stopped at Madgaon, which was the next station, and if so, what was its departure time from that station. He also told him to send a servant to the road with this information. Their move was now beginning to resemble a military operation.

Madgaon was just twenty minutes by train from Vasco. To the general, it made no difference because this whole effort to catch the *Goa Express* at Madgaon seemed quite impossible, but he remained quiet. He had nothing better to offer, so he left it to the colonel to do whatever he thought was best.

Meanwhile, their car was going at breakneck speed through the villages en route. Goans are easy-going people who believe that anything and everything can be happily postponed to the next day, the day after or whenever. This runaway car was something else; it seemed to be in a terrible hurry. Farmers tilling their fields could be seen shading their eyes to look at this strange, speeding apparition that was leaving clouds of dust and squawking chickens in its wake.

They slowed down at the colonel's village to talk to the servant who was waiting on the road. She said that the train was scheduled to reach Madgaon at 13.35 hours and would stop there for ten minutes. A quick look at his watch told the general that the *Goa Express* would now be entering

Madgaon station. They were still an hour and a half away from Madgaon.

They resumed their journey with a burst of speed. The outskirts of Panaji, the capital of Goa, saw them weaving in and out of heavy traffic, with angry drivers honking at them for their lack of respect, violations of road etiquette and lack of consideration for others. The colonel was apologetic, but he was determined to catch the train at Madgaon. Etiquette took a back seat in preference to the need for speed and so he pressed on relentlessly.

The road beyond Panaji opened up, and the velocity of the car also picked up considerably. The little Maruti 800 seemed to sense their urgency and kept up at an awesome speed. It hummed and vibrated, indicating its willingness to match the determination of its owner, who was going absolutely flat out.

The general did not want to look at the speedometer. They were really going too fast. But what could he say? Risks were being taken in their interest, which to the general seemed to be a lost mission. He sat contritely next to the colonel trying to screen out the remarks of a distraught wife, whose perfect holiday had been ruined by a careless and thoughtless husband.

The runaway car was now weaving in and out of traffic coming from the opposite direction. This traffic was headed for Panaji, which was to be the centre stage for Goa's New Year's celebrations. The colonel's wife, who hailed from Madgaon, was guiding her husband and offering short-cut alternatives through roads that would be less congested.

The scenery that sped past was picturesque. Whitewashed churches dotted the hillside amid palm trees glistening in the afternoon sun; tavernas alongside the road were filled with tourists sipping cold beer and fishermen were casting star-spangled nets in the creeks that crisscrossed the road, but no one in the speeding car had the time or inclination to take in the scenery. Their basic concern was: Would they catch up with the *Goa Express* at Madgaon? The colonel was doing all he could to make that happen.

Despite all efforts to follow traffic rules, their manoeuvres left in their wake a stream of agitated drivers protesting at the antics of a strange car that seemed to lack road sense, traffic sense, common sense or any sense whatsoever.

The general tried to consider whether there were any alternatives. Travelling in a taxi or a bus from Madgaon to Pune, even if it was available, was quite impossible. A few months earlier, Anjali had broken her knee in an accident, so sitting through a journey for ten to twelve hours—and that too, over the Western Ghats—was just not possible. Besides, there was no direct flight to Pune from Goa in those days—one had to go to Pune via Bombay—and they would have to wait until the next day to take the flight. In any case, he knew that all flights in and out of Goa were fully booked months in advance. There appeared to be no solution to his dilemma and the situation seemed more than hopeless.

All that the general could now do was pray.

He said, 'Lord, I have really made a stupid mistake. But you know I didn't do this on purpose. If we fail to catch this train, we will have a really big problem on our hands. My wife doesn't ask for much, and if we miss this train,

I will have really failed her. Only you can pull me out of this mess. I cannot think of a solution to this problem, but you are God. For you, all things are possible. Please do something.'

With that, the general left the problem in God's hands and turned his attention back to the road. They were now on an open stretch, and the colonel was belting away with all the speed that the little Maruti could work up.

Just as the general was admiring the resilience of the car and the determination of its driver, there was a sudden, shattering noise from the roof, and the car jerked violently. They looked back to check what had happened and saw their luggage strewn all along the road. The speed of the car had been too much for the rope that had secured their luggage. The colonel braked hard, and he and the general ran back along the road to pick up the luggage that had spread over nearly 100 metres. Picking up the luggage and tying it up once again took another precious ten minutes.

There was now absolutely no hope of ever catching up with the Goa Express, which in any case would have left Madgaon nearly an hour earlier. The general wondered whether the Lord was testing his faith or whether He was in a humorous mood and laughing at their antics in trying to do something that seemed absolutely impossible.

The general looked at his watch again. It was now 2.30 p.m. The Goa Express would be close to leaving Goa and entering Maharashtra. However, he persisted in his prayers. He said, 'Lord, the situation is not getting any better. In fact, it is getting infinitely worse. Are you listening to my prayers?'

The runaway car entered Madgaon city around 2.45 p.m., and the colonel was using all his driving skills to weave through the heavy traffic without reducing speed. People were going about their daily tasks oblivious to the problem.

At 3 p.m., the car sailed into Madgaon station and braked in a cloud of dust. The general jumped out of the car and asked a coolie as to where the *Goa Express* was, expecting to be told, faithless as he was, that the *Goa Express* had left Madgaon an hour and a half earlier.

The coolie's reply left the general speechless.

'The *Goa Express* is outside Madgaon station. It has been waiting there for the past two hours.'

Just at that moment, the general heard an announcement on the railway public address system stating that the *Goa Express* would be arriving at Platform Number 2 in just a few minutes.

The general was overjoyed. He thanked the Lord silently. He really was superb!

The colonel felt vindicated. He, too, had done a great job.

The general tried to be nonchalant about the *Goa Express* waiting for them, as though he had expected all along that they would catch the train.

He looked pointedly at Anjali and said, 'Come now, the *Goa Express* is waiting for us at Platform Number 2, and could we please hurry up?' Anjali gave the general a look that said, 'Just wait till we are alone. I will deal with you suitably then.'

For the time being, however, she was relieved and happy. So was the general.

They reached Platform Number 2, and the *Goa Express* was there waiting for them. The general and Anjali entered their coach, placed their luggage on their berths and returned to the platform to thank the colonel and his wife. It was difficult for them to believe that they had actually managed to catch the *Goa Express*.

The general asked the colonel why he persisted in trying to catch a train that, for all practical purposes, had left Vasco da Gama when they were still at their starting point.

The colonel said, 'I don't know. I just felt compelled to get to that train. Even though the chances were bleak, I felt that if I did my best, we would somehow catch the *Goa Express* somewhere.'

The general blessed the determination of Army officers in general, and this particular colonel who did not give up. In the Army, they were taught never to give up, and that is how some of them triumphed while others surrendered. The general recalled what one of his instructors had said to him long ago when putting his batch through a difficult tactical situation. He had said, 'Battles are won or lost in the minds of men before they are won or lost on the ground.'

The general asked the colonel's wife how she felt about the incident. She replied, 'I just prayed hard because I knew how difficult it would be for you if you missed the train.' Anjali just said, 'Me too.'

The general said, 'So there were three of us praying for the same intention. Maybe God found it difficult to turn us down?'

'No, Sir,' said the colonel. 'There were four of us. I was praying too. I just said to God that we were doing our bit and we needed His help to see us through.'

The train's engine whistled, the guard waved his flag and the *Goa Express* left exactly at 3.15 p.m., just as the General had unintentionally predicted the previous day.

Anjali and the general were quiet on the train, each with their own thoughts. Was it really the Almighty that helped them catch the *Goa Express* that day? If so, then they were certainly touched by the hand of God on 30 December 2002, and that was a very sobering thought. The general knew that God was with them every day and all the time, helping them in many ways, but he also knew that people often tend to take Him for granted. His effort on that day, however, was too dramatic to ignore.

When incidents like this happen, faithless as we are, we look for logical or other reasons to explain miraculous moments.

The general is convinced that it was the hand of God that touched them that day. It is left to the readers to arrive at their own conclusions.

Postscript

The general did write to the stationmaster at Madgaon Railway Station and asked him to check his records for the reason why the Goa Express *was waiting outside Madgaon Railway Station for two hours on 30 December 2002. The general received no answer to his query.*

The general had, however, spoken to the passengers who had boarded the train at Vasco da Gama and were on the Goa Express *when it was held up outside Madgaon Railway Station that day. One of the passengers* said he had walked along the track to find out the reason for the long delay. He said he was told that another train had arrived at Madgaon Railway Station at 13.00 hours on that day, just before the arrival of the Goa Express, and the engine packed up after it had stopped for its regulation halt of ten minutes. A replacement engine was called for, but there was a delay due to the non-availability of a replacement crew. Mechanics and electricians were called to work on the engine of the stalled train and all possible checks were carried out. At around 14.30 hours, the engine suddenly came to life. After all tests were carried out, the engine was declared fit, and the train left at 14.50 hours, making way for the Goa Express to enter the station at 15.00 hours.

India is a spiritual country where there is a belief in God and where all religions are respected. It is up to us to have hope, faith and trust in 'the hand of God'.

Destiny

Is destiny a matter of chance or a matter of choice?

The war in the Far East was not going well at all. Headlines in the world's newspapers trumpeted the desperate situation that the Allies in Burma found themselves in during World War II. The Japanese had, in fact, caught the Allies napping! The destruction of the US naval fleet at Pearl Harbour on 7 December 1941 in the Pacific and the sinking of key battleships of the British Navy, HMS *Prince of Wales* and HMS *Repulse* by Japanese torpedo bombers on 9 December 1941 shocked the Allies and the rest of the world. The Japanese occupied the southern part of Indochina[1] and began to sweep everything before them. The domino effect came into play as countries in the Far East began to fall one after another to the Japanese juggernaut.

Hong Kong surrendered on 25 December 1941. In Malaya, the Japanese Army, commanded by General Yamashita, proved unstoppable. Riding on bicycles, the Japanese raced south and, on 31 January 1942, reached the Straits of Johor, which separate Singapore from the mainland. In Singapore, General Percival, the British Commander, had about 83,000 men and 200 guns under his command, as opposed to Yamashita's 30,000. Yamashita's logistical chain was at its breaking point but that did not stop him. His troops crossed the straits on

to the north-western shore of Singapore on the night
of 8–9 February. The initial waves of attacking troops
suffered heavy casualties, but the Japanese had crossed in
force by dawn. On 14 February 1942, Percival surrendered
to Yamashita in the greatest humiliation ever suffered by
British Forces.

The fall of Singapore heralded the Japanese blitzkrieg
into Burma, and the belief in the invincibility of the British
Army was shattered. It was at this time that a myth began
to take shape: that Japanese soldiers were supermen and
nothing could stop them.

British defences in the East had collapsed like a house
of cards, and Rangoon was now under threat. Allied
strategy was based on the false premise that Singapore
was impregnable and Burma was safe, and that nothing
needed to be done to protect them. There were no reliable
land routes over the mountains and jungles separating
Burma from India. The few airfields in existence were
not strategically located. The British Army Headquarters
at Rangoon was an administrative and not an operational
headquarters; therefore, the defence of Burma was on a
very shaky foundation.

The Japanese had air superiority in Rangoon as
compared to Singapore, and their land forces outnumbered
the Allied forces. They had a clear, strategic goal and the
infrastructure to back it up. The Japanese juggernaut
appeared invincible.

At around this time, far away in south India, a different
story had begun to take shape in Velachery, then a small
village on the outskirts of Madras. Airavatha Mudaliar
(named after Indra's celestial elephant) was a humble

farmer from this village. Mudaliar's son, Kuppuswamy, decided that Velachery had no prospects for the education of his children and moved to Saidapet, Madras, where he was appointed as a supervisor in the Military Engineering Service. He was subsequently posted to Bangalore to supervise the construction of Mayo Hall, which was to be the British centre of administration for Bangalore Cantonment.

Sundaram, one of the main characters of this story, was the second son of Kuppuswamy. He initially grew up in Saidapet and later in Ulsoor, Bangalore. An all-round education under the Jesuits at St Joseph's Indian High School had ingrained in him sound knowledge, discipline, ethics, honesty and good character qualities. The school also turned him into an excellent sportsman.

At home, he was brought up on age-old south Indian traditions that taught him to be courteous, considerate and truthful. He was given charge of the family's horse-cart, the ubiquitous *jatka*, as part of his household duties, and as a result, he developed a good understanding of horses.

Moving back to Madras, Sundaram joined Madras Medical College and became the favourite student of the British professor of surgery. He was the goalkeeper for the college football team and he also joined the University Auxiliary Training Corps, which initiated him into the activities of scouting, which soon turned into a passion. All this shaped him for a life in the Army, although at this time he had neither the design nor the inclination.

The class at Madras Medical College had a few girls who always sat in the front benches. One of them was Padma, a girl from Mysore state, studying on a scholarship. Fraternization with girls was frowned upon, and all that Sundaram could do was admire Padma's long tresses from the back of the class. Moreover, her brother, Venkatachalam, their senior in college, kept a strict watch over who his sister met.

Nevertheless, Sundaram and Padma became good friends and their friendship blossomed into a close relationship after they graduated as doctors. The families looked kindly on this friendship and blessed their proposal for marriage. After Sundaram and Padma were married, Padma was posted to the District Hospital in Chickmagalur, in the state of Mysore, where she was the only lady doctor, while Sundaram applied for and was accepted as a doctor in the same hospital.

Sundaram had a busy routine at the hospital, but his heart yearned for something more exciting. His love for outdoor life and adventure made scouting an obsession, and he was happy to pass on his scouting skills to school and college students.

Meanwhile, World War II was gathering momentum and the Allies were having a rough time on the Burma front. One of the fallouts was a great shortage of doctors and nurses. The demand for more doctors and nurses from England was met with the rejoinder that there were none to spare and that India should provide Indian medical personnel for Indian troops, who formed the bulk of the Army in Burma. As a result of this decision, advertisements appeared across all Indian newspapers asking for volunteers to join the Indian Army Medical Corps and the Indian Military Nursing Service.

It was during this period that Sundaram saw an advertisement in *The Hindu* asking for doctors to join the British Indian Army. He felt that this was an excellent opportunity to combine his love for adventure with his profession as a doctor. He consulted Padma, who supported him, and he applied to join the Indian Army Medical Corps. His application was accepted and after a short course, he was posted as the regimental medical officer (RMO) of the 2nd Battalion of the Fifth Gurkha Rifles (Frontier Force).

After tenures at Landi Kotal, the Khyber Pass and Nowshera, this Gurkha battalion had arrived in Secunderabad via its regimental home in Abbottabad. It had reached Secunderabad on 22 October 1941 after a five-day rail journey. Sundaram, his wife Padma and their son Jagdish joined the battalion in early November and became part of the family of 'Second Five'.

Before the battalion arrived in Secunderabad, it had been deployed in a highly malarial zone in the Tochi area of the North-West Frontier Province, and there had been a very high incidence of malaria in the unit. Relapses were now occurring at an alarming rate of more than twenty a day. The matter was so serious that the Divisional Commander stated that unless the situation improved, the battalion would have to be replaced. This was considered a crisis as it involved the reputation of the battalion as well as the regiment.

It was at this time, in early November, that Lieutenant Sundaram had joined the battalion as its RMO. He promptly set about the formidable task of nursing the battalion back to health and achieved remarkable results within the first few days of his arrival. The history of the 2nd Battalion states:

'The debt of gratitude which the Battalion owes to Sundaram thus started so early, was to go on growing throughout the time ahead.'

Around the same time as Sundaram, Krishnamurthy, a doctor from the neighbouring state of Mysore, saw a similar advertisement in the local newspaper asking for volunteers to join the Indian Army Medical Corps. He too volunteered, was accepted and was posted to the Army hospital in Secunderabad.

Sundaram and Krishnamurthy met frequently at the military hospital in Secunderabad and soon became good friends. Krishnamurthy (Krish for short) was not yet married, but he already had a girl in mind: Kamini— the daughter of a family friend. He asked his parents to arrange his marriage with her. He had seen her grow up and he had liked her from afar. In those days, parents chose marriage partners for their children but sometimes, it was possible for children to influence their parents' choice, as was the case with Krish. Both Krish's and Kamini's parents had met and discussed the possibility of marriage. Kamini was shown a photograph of Krish and she liked what she saw. Kamini was flattered that Krish wanted to marry her because he was a handsome man, but she made it clear that she did not want to be hustled into an early marriage.

Krish was twenty-three years old when he qualified to become a doctor. He was now twenty-four. He was hoping to get married as soon as possible, but Kamini was only seventeen. She was studying for a degree in Arts and her parents wanted her to graduate before she got married. That meant that Krish would have to wait for a minimum of two more years until she graduated, which would be sometime around the middle of 1943.

Krish was often over for meals at Sundaram's place, and their friendship developed into a family relationship. Little did Sundaram or Krish dream that their paths would cross again in faraway Burma, and that too in a desperate war against the Japanese.

In late December 1941, Kamini and her family came over for a short holiday to Secunderabad. Kamini's parents were probably curious about how the Army lived. Kamini proved to be a delightful girl, full of fun and with a pleasant disposition. She and her parents got along very well with Krish and the Sundarams, and the few days that they spent together ended all too soon for both Kamini and Krish.

After this visit, Krish could think of nothing but Kamini and their friendship grew rapidly. He visited Kamini's home in Madras often, and it was generally accepted that Kamini and Krish would marry. Krish was always keen on an early wedding and by now, Kamini had changed her mind and become amenable to the idea too. However, the law did not permit marriage until a girl was eighteen, and married accommodation was not available until an Army officer was twenty-five years old. Kamini's parents, in any case, felt that the marriage should not be rushed. So Krish and Kamini had no option but to wait.

New Year 1942 was ushered in with mobilization orders for 2/5 Gurkha Rifles (FF), but the battalion had no idea whether it would be used in Europe against the

Germans or in Burma against the Japanese. It was placed on the order of battle (ORBAT)[2] of the 48 Indian Infantry Brigade. The other two battalions were the 1/3 and 1/4 Gurkha Rifles. So, in essence, by accident or design, it would be a Gurkha brigade.

Although mobilization orders for the brigade had been given, basic support weapons were issued to the battalion only just before it moved by rail from Secunderabad to Madras.

Padma and her son Jagdish, and some of the other officers' families, went along on the military special to Madras to bid farewell to the battalion. While embarking, the mules accompanying the battalion were very skittish and nervous and refused to go up the gangway to the ship. The officers and men of the battalion were amazed to see Sundaram calm the animals down, lead them quietly up the gangway on to the ship and then down into the hold.

With the battalion and Sundaram on board, the SS *Neuralia* finally set sail from Madras at 10.25 a.m. on 25 January 1942 for an unknown destination.

The small group of families that had come to say goodbye looked quite forlorn on the quay, as the SS *Neuralia* cast off its moorings and headed for the open sea to join the rest of the convoy. Padma and the others watched the ships diminish in size until they disappeared over the horizon and all that was left was a blur of smoke, which, after a while, disappeared too.

It was only after the convoy had cleared Madras that the Commanding Officer (CO), Lieutenant Colonel Ronald Cameron, opened the sealed orders given to him before embarkation. From these orders, he learnt that the battalion was bound eastwards for war against the Japanese, that the disembarkation was to be at Rangoon, and that they would come under the General Officer Commanding Burma.

The training in Secunderabad had been based on the type of warfare prevalent in the western desert; and the change in equipment, especially in animal transport, was the first indication that the battalion was headed for a very different type of warfare. Little, if any, thought had been given to jungle warfare, and with the short time available, it became clear that the battalion would have to gain knowledge of this type of fighting during, rather than before, battle.

Upon arrival in Rangoon, orders were received that 48 Brigade would be part of 17 Indian Infantry Division.

The Japanese offensive against Burma began on 19 January 1942. The Japanese 55th Division attacked from across the Siamese border, while the 33rd Japanese Division crossed further north towards the bridge on the Sittang River. Second Five moved from Rangoon on 6 February 1942. On 7 February, it went into bivouac in scrub[3] jungle and trained for jungle warfare. Being next to a lake, the battalion took the opportunity to train in waterman ship, swimming and the making of various types of watercraft from bamboo and improvised material. This training was probably instrumental in saving many lives later on, in operations when crossing the Sittang River.

While advancing up the Burmese hinterland towards the Bilin River, Second Five had numerous encounters with the Japanese. During one skirmish, they captured a Japanese flag, which now lies on the walls of the regimental centre at Shillong.

17 Infantry Division, also known as the 'Black Cat' Division, now had to contend with two Japanese divisions whose troops and formations were well-equipped and trained in jungle warfare. The aim of the Japanese force was to cut off the 17th Infantry Division at Sittang Bridge.

On 21 February 1942, orders were passed that 17 Division would have to withdraw across the Sittang Bridge. Owing to confusion and slow communication, orders were received to move immediately to cross the bridge over the river Sittang at 6 a.m., on 22 February 1942.

When the orders to move finally reached the battalion, they barely had ten minutes to move. Civilian refugees were also on the move and, at some places, the road was completely blocked by them and their bullock carts. To make matters worse, the troops were subjected repeatedly to air attacks by Japanese fighter aircraft. The roads and tracks were a bedlam of mules, bullock carts and civilian refugees, and the troops had to make their way through this turmoil and uproar. The rations had run out and there was no replenishment for the next meal.

The 33rd Japanese Division was racing towards Sittang Bridge from the north, and the Gurkhas were tasked with preventing them from interfering with the move of the 17th Infantry Division towards the bridge.

Around 10.30 a.m., the CO of 2/5 Gurkha Rifles, Lieutenant Colonel Cameron, gave verbal orders to his Company Commanders to remove the enemy from Buddha Hill and Pagoda Hill, the hill features from which the Japanese were obstructing the movement of the Allied troops trying to cross the bridge.

The attack by the Gurkhas began at 11.30 a.m., and the attacking troops were soon involved in bitter fighting. In the meantime, RMO Lieutenant Sundaram established a first aid post on a hill called RAP Hill (Regimental Aid Post Hill), where all the wounded of 2/5 Gurkha Rifles (FF) were collected.

Japanese reinforcements continued to arrive from the north and the tempo of fighting increased. As the Japanese moved closer to the bridge, their artillery began to get more accurate. At 1.30 p.m., the aid post received a direct hit, resulting in heavy casualties. Lieutenant Sundaram behaved magnificently and showed the coolest of courage in rescuing and treating the wounded under fire.

The intensity of fighting increased with the Japanese being reinforced by units of the 33rd Japanese Division, who were thrown into battle as and when they arrived.

The men had had no food since the previous night and very little water, and with the increasing Japanese opposition, casualties kept mounting. It was decided that, at dusk, the battalion should withdraw to a more defensible ridge line. This was accomplished before nightfall, but an hour before the dawn of 23 February 1942, a loud explosion was heard above the tumult of the battle, indicating that the bridge across the Sittang had been destroyed. The impact of this can only be understood if one is able to comprehend the situation as it was on that fateful day, i.e., the major part of a division with all its transport and guns lying on the wrong side of the ruined bridge!

With the destruction of the bridge, there was no question of trying to save guns or transport. The challenge had boiled down to saving as many men as possible, and this could only be done by swimming across the river.

Except for two small dugout canoes, there were no river crafts of any sort. It was clear that all the craft for the crossing would have to be improvised.

Lieutenant Sundaram once again took charge and started working immediately on getting the wounded down to the beach, making rafts and organizing the crossing.

There was no time to waste. All the available men were assembled and Lieutenant Colonel Cameron explained the situation to them. The battalion was surrounded by the Japanese from three sides, but the troops defending the bridge had managed to keep the approach and the exits to the river open. The CO briefed the men with regard to the route to the beach and the method of collecting bamboo from the riverbank for the making of the river-crossing expedients. Sections were to remain together; the withdrawal was to be as quick as possible in small, independent groups, but there was to be no running. They were to improvise their craft on the narrow beach and make their own way across, with swimmers helping non-swimmers. The rendezvous was to be a railway station some distance beyond the river. Faces were set and grim, but there was no panic and the men marched off quietly.

Enemy artillery had set fire to a whole line of Allied motor transport loaded with ammunition. The burning vehicles, the smoke and the sounds of the exploding ammunition added to the noise and confusion of the battle.

Under cover of these explosions, the Gurkhas were able to withdraw towards the river.

Around 3 p.m., the crossing by the men of 2/5 Gurkha Rifles had commenced. Although many men were crossing the river, there was still a large number on the beach preparing river-crossing expedients. The subedar major was sent down to speed up the crossing.

On the beach, Lieutenant Sundaram organized the construction of river-crossing expedients and the loading of the wounded. Finally, all but five of the casualties had already been sent across. He was just finishing an improvised raft from sodden bamboo, a couple of petrol jerry cans and some empty water bottles when a severely wounded CO of a British battalion came to the water's edge. The raft could not take more than two people. One place was given to the British CO and the other to a rifleman of 2/5 Gurkhas. Another rifleman with a shattered arm was also taken. He had to hold on to the raft with his good arm, as his injured arm trailed in the water. One JCO and two badly wounded riflemen had to be left behind as there was no raft to carry them across. It was a difficult decision to make, but those who were taken across were likely to recover, while those left behind were so badly wounded that their recovery was doubtful.

This raft was accompanied by Jemadar Dhirbahadur Gurung, Lieutenant Sundaram and Lieutenant Colonel Cameron. The CO was the only swimmer. The river was so wide that the raft didn't reach the far bank until 6 p.m. Despite not being a swimmer, Lieutenant Sundaram immediately volunteered to return and retrieve the casualties who were left behind. He was politely denied permission. He was awarded a Military Cross (MC) for his conspicuous gallantry over the last two days, and Jemadar Dhirbahadur was awarded the Indian Order of Merit.

Such was the battle at the Sittang Crossing that only a total of 389 officers and men survived, while the battalion lost nearly 400 lives.

The Japanese forces now turned south to Rangoon and made no attempt to follow up on the withdrawal of 17 Infantry Division. Rangoon fell on 9 March 1942. A few days later, Lieutenant General 'Bill' Slim took over command of the newly formed I Burma Corps.

Back in India, the news of the Battle of Sittang caused some concern, especially among the families of the men involved. Padma was relieved to learn weeks later, that her husband, Lieutenant Sundaram, was among the survivors.

Meanwhile, in Secunderabad, Krishnamurthy waited patiently for the day of his wedding. Kamini's parents, however, were beginning to be more than a little apprehensive about Army life, particularly in times of war.

Towards the end of March 1942, the Japanese began to follow up on the withdrawal of the I Burma Corps and 17 Indian Division. The Allied forces finally passed orders that the whole of Burma Corps would withdraw to India. It was a long march over jungle tracks and dusty roads for hundreds of miles. Many battles were fought by 2/5 Gurkhas, and Lieutenant Sundaram faithfully carried out his duties not only as RMO but also as a commander holding defended areas with his 'walking wounded', i.e., those who were wounded but able to handle a weapon in sector defence. In the meantime, he had not only been awarded the Military Cross for gallantry in the face of the enemy but had also been promoted to Captain's rank.

Finally, on 21 May 1942, the eve of the Raising Day of the regiment, the battalion reached Imphal in India, closing the chapter on the first round of the Battle for Burma. The battalion had suffered no fewer than 543 casualties in this short campaign.

The battalion took time to be refitted and brought up to strength with fresh drafts of recruits from the regimental centre. These men had to be trained and made fit for fresh challenges for their return to Burma.

The battalion was in reasonable shape by the end of 1942. Between March and July 1943, they advanced back into Burma and fought magnificently at Tiddim, Stockades, Fort White and Basha Hill, where Havildar Gaje Ghale won a well-deserved Victoria Cross, the highest award for valour in the British Empire.

In March 1943, Captain Sundaram received the order for his posting to a hospital in a rear area of the Burma front so as to give him a break from frontline service. He had been in frontline action continuously for nearly sixteen months. Coincidentally, it was Krish who was to relieve him. Krish was now in a quandary because his marriage to Kamini had been arranged for May that year, which was three months away.

When Krish requested a deferment of his posting order to July 1943, he was informed that this could only happen if Captain Sundaram agreed. Accordingly, a message was relayed to 2/5 Gurkha Rifles and to Captain

Sundaram. The battalion simply did not want to part with Sundaram, and Sundaram was delighted to remain with the battalion, although it continued to be in the thick of the fighting for the recapture of Burma. Captain Sundaram agreed to the deferment of his posting not only so he could remain with the battalion but also because it would give Krish the time he needed for his wedding to Kamini.

Unfortunately for Krish, his posting to 2/5 Gurkha Rifles was cancelled instead of postponed; the shortage of doctors on the Burma front was such that a deferment was not possible at the time. The date of his posting was not changed. He was posted to a field ambulance in 7 Infantry Division instead of 2/5 Gurkha Rifles, and he had to report by 30 March 1943. He was informed that he could apply for leave for his wedding later, when the situation improved.

7 Infantry Division was in Arakan, Burma, and the fierce fighting taking place there was being reported daily in the Indian newspapers. This caused some dismay and apprehension in the minds of Kamini's parents.

Krish and Kamini asked their parents for permission for an early wedding so that they could marry before Krish left for the front.

It was a very awkward situation for Kamini's parents. They consulted the elders in the family, who decided that the wedding should not take place until Krish returned from the war. At best, an engagement ceremony could take place. Kamini's parents conveyed this decision to Krish and Kamini, who were deeply in love by this time. They were very disappointed at this decision, but Kamini's parents were adamant. A quiet engagement ceremony took place before Krish left for Burma.

At the end of March 1943, Krish moved to 7 Infantry Division in Arakan. One battle followed another in quick succession. The situation was such that sanctioning leave for anyone was out of the question. By November 1943, the division was involved in very fierce fighting in the area of Buthidaung and the Ngakyedauk Pass, a maintenance area for the division within which supply depots, ammunition dumps, vehicle parks and field hospitals were located. This later came to be famously known as the 'Admin Box'.[4]

After taking command of the IVth Army, General Slim issued orders prohibiting any further withdrawal. If any of the divisions were cut off, they would have to hold their ground and fight, and he would relieve them by dispatching counterattacking forces and, if necessary, supplying them by air.

The Japanese, however, surprised the Allies. They had wasted no time. On 4 February 1944, they suddenly appeared five to six miles into Arakan, to the rear of the 7th Division, in considerable strength. They were now two to three miles from the Ngakyedauk Pass and the Admin Box, which was not prepared for anything beyond raids.

Field Marshal Slim, in his book, *Defeat into Victory: Battling Japan in Burma and India 1942–1945*, has vividly described what happened subsequently:

> The Japanese attacked Major General Frank Messervey's 7 Indian Infantry Division Headquarters at the Ngakyedauk Pass. They surrounded the division and overran its divisional headquarters. A fierce fight followed amid the bunkers, tents, and trenches of the headquarters and along the jungle tracks around it.

Clerks, drivers, muleteers, orderlies, signallers, and staff officers threw back attack after attack of yelling Japanese soldiers but when Japanese mortars started shelling the area, its defence became untenable. The General Officer Commanding 7 Indian Infantry Division ordered his headquarters to fight its way out to the 'Admin Box.' After destroying documents and equipment they could not take away, they broke out into small groups, one led by the GOC himself. Casualties were heavy but by the evening they were able to establish a working divisional headquarters. The Japanese, however, followed up in strength and now threatened the 'Admin Box'.

The GOC had to call in two infantry battalions from the outlying positions to use as counter-attack troops. Krish was right there in the thick of it. Casualties were pouring in and lying wherever the stretcher-bearers placed them—Sikhs, Gorkhas, Tamilians and Punjabis lay on stretchers in huddled rows, and Krish and the other doctors were operating non-stop, day and night. They operated on the tops of desks and tables, and the sheets were sodden with the blood of the casualties. Water was scarce, painkillers non-existent, and at night, they operated by the light of lanterns.

General Slim states in his description of the infamous Battle of the Admin Box:

The Japanese Commanders had however decided to destroy the 7th Division and to go 'all out' to do it. They wasted no time. As their reinforcements arrived, they were thrown 'pell-mell' into the battle which was later to be called the battle of the Admin Box. The battle now was hand-to-hand and desperate. The weaknesses of the defences of the Admin Box now became all too apparent. Located as it was in a hollow and dominated closely by the surrounding hills on all sides, the situation was made worse because the location was packed with petrol dumps, ammunition points, harbours for mechanical and animal transport and field hospitals. Further, there were not enough combat troops and the defence of the Admin Box became a nightmare for the defenders with a non-stop incessant hail of artillery and mortar shells.

The defences were manned mostly by administrative staff and non-combatants. Yet they held on, determined to destroy the Japanese offensive. British, Indian and Gurkha officers and soldiers fought and died determined not to yield to the overwhelming and superior Japanese force that had surrounded them. But the manner in which they died will always be a blot on the code of conduct of the Japanese Army. Hundreds of Japanese soldiers yelling blood curdling cries broke into the Box and attacked the field hospitals crowded with the wounded. They slaughtered in cold blood the wounded lying on their stretchers. The doctors who were still operating were lined up and shot. The medical orderlies were made to carry the Japanese wounded back and were then murdered too.

A counter-attack the next morning by the Allied troops found the hospital in shambles, with the only survivors being a few wounded men who had rolled into the jungle and pretended to be dead and were able to describe what had happened.

Krish was among the doctors who had been killed in cold blood.

When the news reached India, Kamini was devastated and inconsolable. Padma had all along felt that it would have been better had Krish and Kamini got married before he left for the front. They would have, at least, had a few months of happiness together rather than nothing at all. Kamini subsequently never married. However, the questions that bothered all of them were: What would have happened if Krish had not asked for the deferment of his posting and had relieved Captain Sundaram? Would he have been alive, and would he have been able to come back to marry his beloved Kamini?

Was it a matter of his choice or was it his destiny? Who knows? What can one say?

Captain Sundaram continued to serve with 2/5 Gurkha Rifles (FF) after his posting order to a field hospital was cancelled. The battalion continued to fight the Japanese, and two more Victoria Crosses (VCs) were awarded to its personnel. It is one of the few battalions in the world to have been awarded three VCs in a single campaign, two of which were awarded on a single day! Captain Sundaram, MC, was very proud of his association with 2/5 Gorkhas and the battalion was extremely happy to have had him as their RMO. He was finally posted out in October 1944. The battalion history records that it was a very sad day for them when he left on posting.

Fourteen years later, on 8 June 1958, Hony Captain Gaje Ghale, VC, Subedar Major of 2/5 Gorkha Rifles (FF) attended the passing-out parade at the Indian Military Academy of the 21st Regular and 10th Technical Courses, of which Second Lieutenant Jagdish Sundaram and the author were a part. Hony Captain Gaje Ghale, VC, had been specifically sent to honour the association of the Sundaram family with 2/5 Gorkha Rifles (FF). Captain Sundaram, MC, and his wife Padma were also there to see their son Jagdish awarded the silver medal for being the best gentleman cadet of the 10th Technical Course.

Postscript

Fifty years and one month later, in July 2008, Captain Sundaram's medals were presented to 2/5 Gorkha Rifles (FF) in Ranikhet by his son, Lieutenant General Jagdish Sundaram, PVSM, AVSM, VSM. Colonel Sunith Cardozo, the eldest son of the author and a second-generation officer of the regiment, was the CO of the battalion at the time.

The small world of Captain Sundaram and 2/5 GR (FF) and of his son Jagdish had come full circle!

The Memento

All that glitters is not gold—so they say!

The general looked at the paper in front of him. At the top was a single sentence—*Plans for Retirement*. It was a paper that he had written a long time ago. It was his intention to start a new way of life that would provide him with good money, honestly earned in the business world, which would keep him and his wife well off and give them the wherewithal to travel around the world. His bucket list included Spain, Portugal, the Nordic countries, Alaska, Japan, Hawaii, Finland and Iceland; and doing things such as skydiving, bungee jumping, travelling in hot-air balloons, snorkelling in the waters of the Andaman Islands, diving in the sea off Lakshadweep, watching the Aurora Borealis, reading the great classics, writing stories, drawing, painting, sketching, learning to play a musical instrument and many other things he could never find the time to do while in the Service.

As a way of life, the Army had been great, but with postings to border areas and consequent multiple establishments to maintain, the money was never enough; and he believed that if he improved his educational qualifications, with a little bit of luck, he could land a well-paying job in the corporate sector so he and his wife could live comfortably ever after. He went back to school while still in the Army and acquired a diploma in human resource development, a bachelor's degree in commerce, a master's degree in business management and another in military science.

After retiring from the Army, he applied for jobs in the corporate sector, and several companies initially expressed interest. They were very polite and said they would call and let him know. The general waited but no call came. He wondered what had gone wrong. Apparently, he had the qualifications and the aptitude, but his attempt to land a job in the business world hadn't worked. On the other hand, officers of the rank of colonel were seamlessly entering the corporate sector. He eventually concluded that he was too old to be hired and that offering employment at a lower level would be disrespectful. Offering him a top-level job without prior experience in the civil sector had its risks, and ultimately, the job offers that he hoped for never materialized.

After a while, he finally found his niche when a Delhi NGO approached him to join them in caring for children with disabilities. He had been called to meet the children so that he would get an idea of what was expected of him.

One look at the children and his decision was made. He joined them the next day and settled down comfortably in the world of children with disabilities.

One Thursday morning in November 2004, the telephone operator put through a call to the general and said, 'Call for you, Sir, from some political person.'

Political person? The general wondered who this could be. He picked up the phone and identified himself.

The person at the other end announced who he was and waited for the general's reaction.

The general just said, 'Good morning. What can I do for you?'

The voice at the other end of the line said, 'Do you know who I am?'

The general answered, 'You just told me who you are.'

The speaker didn't seem to be too happy with the general's response and said, 'Have you heard of me before?'

The general truthfully said, 'No.'

The political person handed the phone to one of his staff members, who said, 'Sir, you were just speaking with the General Secretary of the National Party for Democracy. Would you like to meet him today at 11 a.m.?'

The general was beginning to get mystified. The person at the other end of the phone seemed to suggest that it was the general who wanted to see this political person, which was not the case, but it was possible that the person speaking to him at the moment could not express himself appropriately. The general, however, did not want to appear rude, so he said, 'I do not know what this is all about. Does the General Secretary of the National Party of Democracy want to meet me?'

'Yes, yes,' the voice said. 'At your office, at 11 a.m.' That made the situation a little clearer.

The general checked the planner on his desk and it indicated that he was free that morning. However, he would need permission from the director of the NGO to meet with someone political on a matter that was not yet clear. The general said, 'Please give me your contact number and I will call you back.'

After obtaining permission from the director to meet this person, the general rang back and said, 'Yes, the appointment has been cleared for 11 a.m. Does the General Secretary have a bodyguard?'

'Yes,' replied the voice at the other end, and added very importantly, 'Commandos! Black Cat Commandos! Four of them!'

The general was unimpressed and replied in a very matter-of-fact tone, 'Well, he will have to leave the commandos in the parking area. We cannot have them inside this institute. We care for disabled children here, and they may possibly get alarmed with armed commandos moving around with weapons.'

There was some muted conversation at the other end, after which the person agreed to leave the commandos in the car park.

The General Secretary of the National Party for Democracy arrived at the institute at precisely 11 a.m. He had three people with him other than the commandos, who were left outside. They were escorted to the general's office by one of the security guards of the institute.

It was break time for the children and they were playing outside on the lawns. Contrary to the general's fears, the children had eyes only for the commandos! They crowded around them and were happily asking them all sorts of questions. The commandos were equally happy to be with the children. It must have been a welcome change for them, considering the type of people they normally met in connection with their security duties.

The General Secretary was slim, trim and meticulously dressed. Unlike the general look of most politicians, he was dressed in a smart safari suit. He walked with a limp and carried an elegant silver-topped walking stick. He explained the limp by saying that there had been an attack on his life and he had been injured, hence the stick.

The general now remembered 'the man and the attack on his life because of a particularly gory newspaper photograph of a policeman carrying a head that had been severed from one of the victim's bodies. The whole incident now came back to the general, as did the fact that the General Secretary was a brave man who had continued with his work despite the threat to his life. The general was now beginning to feel glad that he was meeting with this man, who was committed to his ideals and a cause larger than himself.

The general's office was quite small, but he managed to fit the four of them in.

The General Secretary was very polite; he introduced himself and said that he had heard about the general and had even read and liked one of his books, *Param Vir*. He went on to say that he was there to personally invite the general to a function he was organizing at Vigyan Bhavan. The function was to honour people who had done something good for the nation in war and peace, and the general was one of them. There would be a group of eminent people on the dais to grace the occasion, and it would consist of ex-prime minister Narasimha Rao, the politician Amar Singh, film stars Amitabh and Jaya Bachchan, industrialist Anil Ambani and his wife Tina, the CEO of Sahara Airlines and some others. He added that he was there personally because the function was only a few days away and he needed immediate confirmation from the general.

The general was more than a little mystified as to why, of all people, he wanted him to be there as well.

The General Secretary seemed to read the general's thoughts and said, 'I consider you to be a war hero, Sir, and would like to honour you, as well as some other service personnel and civilians who have done much for the country but have never been suitably rewarded.'

The general replied, 'Soldiers do not look for rewards. All that we look forward to is the respect of the people of India for the work that we do to keep them safe.'

The General Secretary answered. 'General, that is the problem with you soldiers. You make all the sacrifices but you do not look for rewards, and that is why you do not receive them. Your status, pensions and salaries are a case in point. I am trying to make up for this in my own way. As a member of Parliament, I receive a grant for the people of my constituency, and it is my endeavour to pick those who, in my opinion, have done something for the people of India, and this is my way of expressing the nation's gratitude.'

He continued, 'I have also been particularly impressed by the poem in your book about the 'Unknown Soldier'. I would like you to read out the poem at the function. Hopefully, it would make more people understand the need for a national war memorial, which is what the poem is all about. There will be over 2000 people at Vigyan Bhavan listening to you.'

'And,' he added, 'may I have twenty-five copies of your book? I would like to give them to the VIPs attending the function.'

The general was delighted that twenty-five more people would read his book. He told the General Secretary that he could get them directly from his publisher and shared the address and telephone number.

The general also confirmed that he was happy to accept the General Secretary's invitation to be present at the function at Vigyan Bhavan.

With that, the General Secretary and his team got up and left.

On the appointed day, the general put on his regimental blazer and tie and drove off to Vigyan Bhavan in his old Maruti 800. He was met at the gate by a security person, who got into his car and guided him to the VVIP parking area.

The cars in the parking lot were all the latest models, shining and resplendent in the late afternoon sun. The general's Maruti looked like a relic among those state-of-the-art cars.

There was also a large number of buses in a corner of the parking area.

The escort guided the general into the auditorium of Vigyan Bhavan and the latter was surprised to find that it was already packed. He then realized that the buses in the parking area were the vehicles that had been commandeered to bring the audience to the venue. The auditorium seats approximately 2000 people.

The general was taken to the front row and placed between two people whose faces seemed vaguely familiar. He learnt that one was a cricketer whose name had been cleared from some match-fixing scam, and the other was a middle-distance runner who had been under a cloud for allegedly taking prohibited drugs that enhanced her performance but had now been exonerated.

The general wondered how he came to be included in such august company!

After a while, some members of the audience began lining up to take autographs from the people on the general's right and left. A few of them looked at the general, decided that he was not worth the trouble and walked away.

Suddenly, the audience rose to their feet and began cheering and clapping. The general looked towards the stage, where he saw former prime minister Narasimha Rao, Amitabh Bachchan, Jaya Bachchan and the other VIPs. They waved back at the crowd and there was much shouting and cheering.

By this time, the general realized that the audience was not the type to understand his poem at all and, therefore, would not be able to appreciate it. He had heard about how people were brought by busloads for political functions and wondered whether this was one of them. He began to wish that he had brought along the Hindi translation of his poem instead of the English version. However, it was too late, and there was nothing he could do about it. He was quite sure that there would be ominous silence after he had read his poem, and he knew that he would feel quite diminished as and when that happened.

While he was busy with these thoughts, the general noticed the General Secretary talking to some of the VIPs on the stage and pointing at him. Soon, some of the dignitaries came down from the stage with their copies of his book to get them autographed by him. The general began to feel a little better.

The function began. The General Secretary addressed the crowd and explained the reason for the function. The general heard his name mentioned in connection with the Bangladesh War and his book. He spoke about each of those who were being honoured in turn. He also spoke about a captain, who the general now noticed, sitting a row behind him. He smiled and waved when he noticed that the general was looking at him. The general waved back. He was glad to know that there was another *fauji*[1] along with him. The general also learnt from the General Secretary's speech that the widow of one of the Param Vir Chakra awardees was also present at the function.

The general's turn to read the poem was announced. He climbed up the steps to the stage and faced the vast concourse of faces. He wondered what would happen. He started to read the poem. He knew it by heart, so he kept looking at the faces in the audience while reciting it. Their faces were blank and unreadable. His heart sank.

The general stepped back from the rostrum as soon as he finished reciting the poem.

To his astonishment, 2000 small national flags were being waved furiously, and people were clapping and cheering madly. He just couldn't understand the sudden transition from blank faces to exuberant cheering.

The general got down from the stage and went back
to his seat, feeling most relieved and at the same time very
perplexed.

Mr Narasimha Rao took the rostrum next. As he
proceeded with his speech, the crowd enthusiastically
waved their flags and cheered at just the right places. The
general looked at the stage and saw one of the organizers
standing behind the VIPs.

The VIPs couldn't see him but the audience could.

The man had a small national flag in his hand. Each
time a clap or a cheer was required, he would wave his flag
and the audience would respond by waving their flags in
return and cheering enthusiastically. They seemed to be
enjoying this game and everyone was happy—the crowd,
the speakers and the organizers.

The general realized why they had cheered for him too,
but he felt grateful.

It was finally time for the distribution of awards. Mr
Rao came forward to make the presentations and the
emcee began to read out the names. The first name to be
read out was that of the cricketer and everyone cheered.
Next was the athlete and there was more cheering. The
widow of the Param Vir Chakra recipient was next. Each
of them received a small memento and a cheque.

The cricketer received a cheque for Rs 11 lakh,
the middle-distance runner was handed a cheque for
Rs 8 lakh, and the widow was given a cheque for
Rs 10 lakh. The general was amazed at the distribution
of these amounts of money. He concluded that, being a
member of Parliament, the General Secretary had money
to spend on his constituency, and perhaps he had made

all of them his constituents. The general considered it to be good for them and wondered how much money he and the captain would receive! Some more names were called out. Each of them received a cheque for varying amounts.

It seemed to the general that the armed forces personnel had been kept for last. He remembered that some people always save the best for last. He wondered whether the size of the cheque would also be the best. He could not help wondering how much that would be. He began making plans for how he would spend the money.

At last, his name was announced.

The general went up to the stage and two men came forward carrying a huge memento in a glass case. Inside the glass case were what looked like two huge stainless steel daggers with brass handles that crossed diagonally, with a big brass Ashoka lion emblem placed in the space in between. The daggers were mounted on a solid brass platform, on which there was some inscription. There was a lot of cheering from the audience.

The memento was too heavy for Mr Rao to lift, so he just touched it. The general did the same. The two men carried it back and placed it on a table at the back of the stage. There was no cheque!

The general returned to his seat feeling very disappointed. He then remembered his wife's advice to him. 'Never expect anything from anyone. Whatever you receive, treat it as a bonus, and you will never be disappointed.'

Captain Sharma was called next. He too was presented with a similar memento. There was no cheque for him either.

The General Secretary then came forward to thank everyone. The function had come to a close. The VIPs on the stage got up and waved to the crowd. Amitabh Bachchan was the star attraction. The crowd cheered loudly.

The general made his way to one of the exits.

Captain Sharma came across to meet him and asked, 'Sir, why were we not given cheques?'

The general replied, 'I don't know, and I don't intend to ask!'

At that moment, one of the men on the General Secretary's staff came across to say that the General Secretary had requested the general to stay back as he wished to speak with him regarding something important. The general sat down near one of the exits.

Captain Sharma took the man aside and started speaking with him. He came to the general after the man had gone away and said that he had asked him why they had not been treated in the same manner as the others and not been given cheques. He said that the person concerned did not know but that the General Secretary would probably explain.

The General Secretary took a long time to come and the general began to get restless. He had a dinner appointment that evening, where he was the host, so he sent word to the General Secretary's staff officer to say that he could not wait much longer and needed to leave.

The staff officer rushed over to apologize to the general and ask that he stay back, as the General Secretary was seeing off the VVIPs and would not be too long.

The general informed the officer that he could not wait as he had a dinner appointment that evening and, as the host, he could not keep his guests waiting.

The general then got up to leave.

'What about the memento?' the staff officer asked.

The general explained that he could not take it, as the memento was too heavy to carry and also too large for his small flat.

The staff officer was visibly upset and said, 'Sir, that will be a big insult to the chairman and to our society.'

Just then, another emissary arrived with a message requesting the general to please wait as the General Secretary would be with him in a few minutes.

After waiting another ten minutes, the general insisted he really had to go and got up to leave.

After the general had made it quite clear that he was leaving, two men appeared carrying the memento and accompanied the general to his car, where they managed to just about fit it into the boot of his Maruti 800. When the general shut the door of the boot, the top of the memento was touching the roof of the car. It was that big!

The general drove home, wondering what his wife would say when she saw the huge object.

The general's wife was waiting for him at home, upset at having to wait for such a long time and worried that their guests would arrive before them. He picked her up and they drove off to the United Service Institution, which was where they were hosting the dinner. While driving, he told her what had transpired at the Vigyan Bhavan function but she wasn't interested in listening to any of it. All that she was interested in was being at the venue before her guests arrived.

They arrived at the Pavilion, at the United Service Institution of India, where the dinner was being held, just a few minutes ahead of their first guests.

After dinner and seeing off their guests, the general walked his wife to the rear of the car to show her the memento. She was taken aback by its size. It was a full moon night, and the swords, the huge Ashoka emblem and the brass platform shone like burnished gold and silver in the bright moonlight.

The general's wife asked, 'What do you intend to do with this memento and where will you keep it? It certainly can't come into the house.' The general answered, 'I do not know. We will have to let it remain in the car for the time being.'

The next morning, when he was leaving for work, he found a crowd of people from the colony standing at the back of the car and peering at the memento.

The memento remained in the car for a few days, as there was absolutely no place for it in the flat. Whenever he went to the car, there would always be someone looking at it.

After a week, the general decided to keep the memento in his office at the NGO where he worked. He placed it on the top of his small Godrej steel cupboard, where it remained for some years.

The general subsequently changed jobs and began working for war-disabled soldiers, and he forgot all about the memento. One day, he received a telephone call from the administrative supervisor of the NGO where he had previously worked, informing him that during the whitewashing of the office, the glass cover of the memento had got damaged. The supervisor further requested the general to take the memento away as the new incumbent of the office wanted it removed.

The general explained that there was no place for the memento at his home and requested the supervisor keep it in one of their storage spaces for the time being. The supervisor was kind enough to agree, and the memento was placed in a storage area for a while, gathering dust along with broken-down wheelchairs, walkers and crutches.

A year later, the general received a call from the captain who had also been present at the Vigyan Bhavan function. He had become a major and was home on leave from wherever he was posted.

'Good morning, Sir,' he said. 'Major Sharma here. Do you remember me? We were at the Vigyan Bhavan function a few years ago, where we were given those huge mementoes. I was a captain at that time. I just wanted to ask you whether you still have the memento with you.'

The general replied, 'No, but I know where it is.'

He said, 'Good. That's great!' Then he added, 'I was offered Rs 3 lakh for my memento, but I bargained with the buyer and he has given me Rs 5 lakh for it.'

'Rs 5 lakh!' exclaimed the general. 'Who is the buyer?'

'He is a real estate dealer from Gurgaon,' he replied.

'Why is he offering so much money for the memento? He must be crazy!'

'He said that there are only two or three of its kind and that there is a foreign buyer.'

'How does he know that there are only two or three such mementoes?' the general asked. 'And as you and I know, there are actually only two of their kind in existence, and they are not antique, so they have no historical value either. There must be something more to it. Why don't you try to find out?'

'Sir,' Major Sharma replied. 'What's the point? If we are getting good money for it, why should we care? It's a perfectly legitimate deal. We have something, and someone wants to buy it, so why ask too many questions'? What I want to tell you is that you should try to negotiate for a better price and see what he says. May I give him your name and telephone number?'

The general said, 'Yes, of course, but could you find out a little more about this?'

'Okay, Sir, I'll try,' the major replied.

With this, the general hung up and called the NGO where the memento was stored. Once again, he forgot his wife's advice and started making plans for what he would do with the money. Buying a new car was a priority on his agenda.

The general finally got through to the NGO and inquired about the whereabouts of his memento. No one seemed to know! There had been a number of changes in the staff over the years, and the present lot had not even heard of the memento. The general decided to speak to the director, whom he knew well and felt sure that she would know. However, she was away.

The general began to get a little apprehensive about the memento, which he had neglected for so many years and which suddenly seemed to have become precious and had taken on a new life.

He decided to visit the NGO the next day to locate his memento. That evening, he managed to speak with the director. She remembered the memento and promised to find out where it was.

The next day, when the general went to meet the director, she ordered tea for both of them and said, 'I recall very well the huge memento that was lying in your office. I also recall ringing you up a number of times to ask you to take it away, and you finally requested that we put it in storage. It was placed in a storage space at the rear of our buildings, which housed old wheelchairs and junked metal appliances. Some time ago, the fire brigade authorities sent us a notice saying the space was badly located, as it would obstruct the movement of fire engines in the event of a fire. They said the space would have to be demolished, failing which we would not be given fire services clearance.

'Therefore, I asked the administration supervisor to demolish the storage space. He wanted to know what was to be done with the disused items lying there, and I asked him if they were of any use to us. He said, "No." So, I told him to get rid of them, little realizing that your memento was lying there too. A scrap metal dealer was called, and all the items were properly weighed and sold. I'm afraid your memento was sold too, along with the rest of the scrap metal.'

The general's heart sank.

She continued, 'I have requested the file from Administration, which has details of the sale of the scrap metal. I found that your memento was weighed separately and fetched a price of 300 rupees. The person who conducted the scrap metal sale had no idea that the memento belonged to you and no one mentioned it to me either. So, we owe you 300 rupees. I'm sorry for the delay.' After saying this, the director pushed three crisp hundred-rupee notes across the table.

The general did not know what to say. His memento, for which he had no time and the going rate for which was approximately Rs 5 lakh or more, was sold for just Rs 300!

'Could you please check whether there is a phone number on the sales receipt and give it to me?' the general asked, thinking he could perhaps buy it back.

The receipt did have a telephone number. The general called the number, but there was no response. Then he called the telephone company's complaints department and was told that the number was no longer in use.

The general called Major Sharma and told him what had happened. He also asked for the telephone number of the real estate dealer who wanted to buy the memento.'

Major Sharma said, 'It is strange that he has not yet spoken to you. He was so keen to meet up with anyone who had a similar memento. However, I have his telephone number. Here it is.'

The general called the number. A clerk of the real estate agent answered, said that the agent was out of town and asked if he could be of help in any way.

The general asked for the office address and was told it was in Gurgaon. Major Sharma said he knew where the real estate agent's office was located and offered to go there and unobtrusively find out why the owner was offering such a huge amount for the mementoes.

Major Sharma called the next day and reported: 'I met up with the staff at the real estate office and none of them volunteered to talk. However, one of them, apparently a disgruntled worker, rang me up later and agreed to meet me. He thought that I was an income tax officer! I did not divulge who I was'.

'The person said that the owner was initially a scrap metal dealer and that one day he had a windfall when some objects fell into his hands that turned out to be pure gold and silver. He managed to sell them at a very high price and used the money to buy land in Gurgaon, which he resold at a profit. Then with part of the proceeds, he set up this real estate business, which is now thriving.'

Major Sharma added, 'It is now clear why the real estate agent did not ring you. Your name was on the memento that he had bought as scrap. So, when I gave him your name, he realized that there was no point in ringing you because he already had your memento, on which he had made such a huge profit. You are the last person in the world that he would have liked to meet!'

Sometime later, the general met the staff officer of the politician and told him what had happened. The staff officer said, 'The General Secretary wanted very much to talk with you about the memento but you did not wait. He felt offended when he heard that you had gone away and decided not to communicate with you further on the subject.'

The general asked, 'Why did the General Secretary go through so much trouble to make the memento with such precious metals when he could have avoided all this effort by just giving us cheques?'

His answer had the general stumped. He said, *'General Secretary ne socha ki fauji log ko paisa dena apman hai.'* (The General Secretary felt that it would be disrespectful to give money as an award to soldiers.)

The general eventually met the real estate agent who had profited from the purchase and sale of his memento. The man admitted to buying an object that was sold to him as scrap metal, which he reconditioned and sold at a profit. He said that it was a perfectly legitimate deal, that he had the receipt for the money that he had paid and that he owed the general nothing.

He had, in fact, done his homework well and knew that it was a legitimate deal.

The general could do nothing about it. He realized too late that the saying, *'All that glitters is not gold'* may not always be true!

Postscript

The belief, by some, that soldiers should not be compensated with money and that honour is enough leaves soldiers with honour intact but nothing in their pockets!

Ward No. 21

To fear love is to fear life, and those who fear life are already three parts dead

—Bertrand Russell

Major General Simranjeet Singh, Commandant of the Command Military Hospital, looked at the vista stretching into the distance beyond the tall Ashoka trees delineating the boundary of the upper officers' ward. It was still dark, and all that she could see were a few lights in the pre-dawn darkness of a sleepy Pune on an early Sunday morning.

Simran had gone for her regular early morning walk, when on an impulse, she turned into the hospital and walked towards the upper officers' ward. The nurse on night duty, who was writing her patient reports, was startled to see the Commandant making an unscheduled and unannounced appearance. That too, so early on a Sunday morning! She wondered what was wrong.

Simran put her at ease, saying that she just wished to sit in a corner of the veranda of the upper officers' ward for a while. She had promised herself that she would do this on the day she assumed command of the hospital, and that was three years earlier. Somehow, she hadn't found the time to carry out her wish. This was her last opportunity to fulfil this long-standing desire of hers, as she would be handing over the hospital to the new Commandant in a few days. She instructed the duty nurse that she was not to be disturbed, except in an emergency, as she just wanted to be left alone for a while.

It was her wedding anniversary, and she wanted an opportunity to walk down memory lane, but she didn't tell the duty sister that.

The veranda where she was sitting ran along the rooms of a new wing that was added after the Sino–Indian War of 1962, when the hospital authorities realized the need for additional space to accommodate the huge influx of battle casualties during a war. The rooms were no longer new, but when compared to the main hospital buildings that were over 150 years old, these rooms were considered quite modern. There were ten rooms in all, each with an attached bathroom. The first two rooms were subsequently converted into a VIP room for senior battle casualties, and the third into a dressing room for treating patients within the ward. The veranda angled off to the left of the VIP room and the dressing room, giving some privacy to those rooms. To the left, in a straight line, were rooms numbered 4 to 10.

Simran pulled up a chair and sat in front of the VIP room, which was unoccupied, and contemplated the scene before her. The morning star shone brightly in the sky and a cool breeze wafted in from the east, bringing with it the fragrance of jasmine from the shrubs beyond the lawn. The breeze and the fragrance of the jasmine flowers triggered memories of earlier days spent on this veranda and the events that led to her coming to Pune so many years ago.

She had first come to this officers' ward thirty years earlier. She was just a college girl then, running away from an arranged marriage.

She had returned to her home in Delhi one evening to find her parents entertaining some people she had never seen before. A pale blue Mercedes was parked outside the house, with a liveried chauffeur standing by. As she entered the living room, the ongoing conversation stopped and all eyes turned towards her. She folded her hands in a 'namaste' and proceeded to her room. Her mother followed her, asking her to wash up and come out to meet the guests. Simran didn't like the look of the visitors and did not want to go out to meet them. She intuitively knew that this meeting was about a proposal for her marriage, and she didn't want to take this matter any further. She was still talking with her mother when her father entered her room and brusquely told her to 'Behave and come out immediately' to meet those people, as it was for her own good.

Simran was filled with a sense of foreboding and did not want to be trapped in a situation she would find difficult to get out of. She also knew that her father was a tyrant and had witnessed his treatment of her mother over the years. She knew instinctively that any link with the people sitting outside would be a repetition of her mother's life. Her eyes welled up with tears, but she knew that her father was in no mood to brook any opposition. Her mother wiped away her tears and they went to the living room. Simran sat on a chair kept vacant for her and she could feel the eyes of the visiting trio minutely inspecting her. There was an awkward silence, which was broken by her father, who introduced his guests.

Mr Khanna, he said, was in the import and export business and had his main office in Delhi at Connaught Place. He had started the business a decade earlier, expanded it to many times its initial turnover and added branch offices in Mumbai, Madras and Calcutta. He was a self-made man, and because he contributed money to carefully chosen institutions, he had become an important member of Delhi society. He was assisted in the initial stages by Mrs Khanna, who helped him start the business. Now that the business was on a firm footing, she had the time to be part of a number of lady's clubs. Their son, Deepak, had just earned his master's degree in management and was being groomed to take over his father's business. They also had a daughter, who had not accompanied them that day, and they were looking for a daughter-in-law who would, with the heir apparent, take the business to greater heights.

Simran had no desire to be part of this family and sat with downcast eyes. She, however, also realized that such a demeanour would present the Khannas with the image of the demure bahu, which was certainly not the impression that she wanted to convey, so she looked up at these people who had come to see her.

Mr Khanna had obviously been enjoying the fruits of the profits of his business. His belly spilled over the belt that held up his trousers. Hair grew unbridled out of his ears and his moustache covered his upper lip. His lower lip hung loose, displaying yellow teeth stained brown with betel nut. Shaggy eyebrows matched the hair growing out of his ears, and his small, black eyes failed to conceal a shrewd and crafty personality. Strangely, although he was so hairy, his head was devoid of any hair. His fat fingers, which were clasped across his belly, had an array of gold rings with different coloured stones. Fortunately, he did not do the talking.

Mrs Khanna matched her husband in corpulence. Her hair was cut short and dyed. The colour of her hair did not match the age lines on her heavily made-up face. Her painted lips were thin and inclined downwards. The painted nails on her hands and feet were long and pointed. She was a very unprepossessing woman, to say the least.

Deepak was a younger version of his father.

Simran wondered how and where her father had picked up this lot and was extremely upset with him for trying to arrange her marriage into this family.

Mrs Khanna spoke. 'Beta,' she rasped in a throaty voice, 'we hear that you have just finished your BSc exams and that the results are going to be out in a few days. Are you planning to study further, like getting a degree in management or something like that?'

The obvious inference was, 'If you are thinking of further studies, you should get your MBA as that would help the business.' Simran decided to put an end to this trend of thought and replied, 'No ji, I am planning to do my MBBS. I want to become a doctor.'

Mrs Khanna was taken aback and looked at Simran's father as if to ask, 'So, where do we go from here?'

Offended by his daughter's answer, Simran's father said, 'Simran is considering various options. She has not yet made up her mind. Doing her MBA is very much an option.'

Mrs Khanna smirked and Mr Khanna displayed his approval with a smile. Deepak looked unhappy. Simran's mother seemed sad and uncomfortable. Simran was annoyed and upset.

Mrs Khanna began talking about the rapidly expanding family business and their plans to grow it further, about the property they owned, about their connections with politicians and senior bureaucrats and about her social circle. Simran's father kept nodding in approval. Deepak kept looking vacantly in front of him—he didn't seem to have a mind of his own.

Simran's mother made the tea and passed the cups around. Out of courtesy, Simran served the biscuits. 'Thank you, beta,' said Mr Khanna, looking Simran up and down. Mrs Khanna and Deepak said, 'No, thank you,' but gave her the 'once over' as well. Mrs Khanna continued her monologue about the merits of her family, the business and her social circle until it was time for them to leave.

After they left, Simran's father upbraided his daughter. 'Why were you so cold to our honoured guests?' he asked. 'Do you have no regard for your parents' wishes? Aren't you aware that we are doing this for your own good?'

Simran plucked up the courage to answer her father. 'Papa, if it is my good that you are seeking, don't you think that my wishes need to be considered and that I should be asked what I want in life?'

'Since when do your wishes count? Did your mother or I ever have any choice in such matters? Since when have you become so insolent? You will do what we tell you and push this foolish notion of becoming a doctor out of your head. You belong to a business family, and the union of our family with the Khannas will bring great prosperity to both families.'

Simran replied, 'Papa, if it is your business that you are thinking about, then please keep me out of it.'

Simran's father was furious. 'Go to your room and stay there,' he said. Turning to his wife, he added, 'It is you who has put all these foolish ideas into her head.'

Simran, who was confined to her room, could hear her father yelling at her mother and berating her for her daughter's attitude.

Simran now recollected the scene as if it had happened just yesterday.

Simran's parents were aware that she was friendly with Ashok, a young officer of the Indian Army. Simran and Ashok had grown up together and had gone to the same neighbourhood school. Her mother liked the young officer, but her father did not approve. He felt that Army officers were an impoverished lot and what mattered to him was money. He had warned Simran against continuing her relationship with Ashok but she continued to see him. Then the 1971 War broke out, and Ashok went with his battalion to the front in Jammú and Kashmir.

Simran made daily visits to the mandir to pray for Ashok's safety. She often met his mother there, who brought her up to date on news about Ashok. His battalion was involved in the fighting, and there had been no news from the front for a while. Then, one day, Ashok's mother conveyed the news that he had been wounded but did not know how serious it was. Subsequently, Simran found out that Ashok's right leg had been amputated and that he had been evacuated to a military hospital in Udhampur. She was told later that Ashok had been taken to the Command Hospital in Pune, where he would be fitted with an artificial leg at the Artificial Limb Centre (ALC). Simran's family learnt of Ashok's injury as they lived in the same neighbourhood. Simran's mother felt sad for Simran and Ashok, but her father was happy because he felt that this would put an end to the relationship between his daughter and the officer.

He thought since Ashok was now disabled, he would have no future and could probably be forced to leave the Army, and that in such circumstances, his daughter would no longer be interested in pursuing the relationship. Strangely, even though he was her father, he did not know his daughter and failed to realize that this would only bring Ashok and Simran closer to each other.

Sometime after Ashok reached Pune, he wrote to Simran and told her about what had happened. He also suggested that things should change between them now that he had lost a leg. This made Simran very angry, and she replied, saying that nothing of the sort would happen and that nothing could ever come between them.

As Simran sat in the veranda, she went over the trauma of those days and its effect on her young heart and mind. It was still dark outside, but there were now pink tints in the sky, heralding the coming dawn. A rooster called from a household beyond the boundary wall of the officers' ward to announce a new day, and crows called sleepily from somewhere beyond the lawn.

Simran remembered how much she had wanted to visit Ashok in Pune and reassure him that her love for him would never diminish, but getting away from home was impossible. Ashok called her from a public phone booth located a kilometre away from the hospital, whenever he could get away from the ALC, and he gave her the telephone number of the officers' ward. But that phone was invariably busy except at night, and talking at night was not possible for Simran because her father was at home. Therefore, their communication was restricted to letters.

In the meantime, Simran appeared for the All India Medical Examination for entrance to a medical college. She also took the Armed Forces Medical College entrance examination. She was pleased with her performance at both examinations and was eagerly awaiting the results. Her mother had signed all the application forms.

A month after the visit from the Khannas, Simran's father returned home earlier than expected. It was a phone call from the Khannas that had prompted him to come home early. They had apparently liked Simran and wished to set a date for the engagement, and they wanted it soon. So he came home to decide on a suitable date. Simran had gone to college and her mother was at the dentist. Mr Khanna wandered around the house with nothing to do and he came across a letter on the sideboard. It had Simran's name and address on it. He flipped the envelope over to see if the sender's name was written on the back, but it was blank. He weighed the envelope in the palm of his hand, wondering where it had come from. Curiosity got the better of him and he decided to investigate. The privacy of his daughter's correspondence was not a concern for him. He slit the envelope open.

The letter was from Ashok, and the contents infuriated him.

Simran and her mother reached home simultaneously and were welcomed with a blistering salvo from her father. Waving the letter and shouting at the top of his voice, he accused both mother and daughter of conspiring against him and charged them with disloyalty, disrespect and disobedience. He raved, ranted and cursed. Simran's mother wilted under the verbal onslaught of her husband.

Simran tried to protect her mother but this only infuriated her father further.

Simran, however, had had enough. She said, 'Papa, Mama has nothing to do with this, and you had no right to open my letter. Please give it to me.'

Her father was now shaking with rage. 'Privacy?' he shouted. 'What privacy? You are my daughter, and as long as you are in my house, you have no right to carry on a relationship with anyone without my permission. You have disobeyed my orders by continuing your friendship with this one-legged fellow when you are aware that we have other plans for your marriage.'

Simran was now just as enraged as her father. She matched her father's tantrum with cold logic. She said, 'Papa, you forget that I am nineteen years old. I am an adult. I can choose my own friends and I don't need your permission.'

This was more than her father could stand. 'As long as you are in my house, you will do as I say,' he said, roughly grabbing her arm, pushing her into her room and shutting the door.

Simran was devastated. She realized that her father would force her to marry Deepak Khanna. She had gathered from her father's outburst that the Khannas were pressing for an early engagement, and that every moment she spent at home would now bring her closer to the disaster that awaited her.

Simran ran away from home early the next morning. She was gone when her father awoke.

Simran's father's anger had now turned to cold rage. Simran had written a note to her mother, which was recovered by her father from the servant even before her mother could read it. He immediately rang up a friend in the police and asked for help in framing a First Information Report (FIR). He also rang up friends with political connections to help him pursue the case.

The FIR stated that his daughter was kidnapped by a Major Ashok Kumar of the Indian Army, who was now at the ALC in Pune, and asked that the officer be immediately arrested and his daughter returned to him.

Simran recalled that on that day, she had no plan other than escaping from the clutches of her father. She walked along the roads and streets of Delhi without any aim or sense of direction until she felt that she needed a cup of tea. It was early in the morning, and Delhi was just waking up. She looked at the signboards of the shops for a clue as to where she was and found that she had reached Lajpat Nagar. She entered a bylane and found a small restaurant. All she had on her was the bag she usually carried to college. She checked her purse and realized that she would need more money. She had a savings account with the bank at her college, so she decided to go there. After drinking her tea, she called for an autorickshaw, went to the bank at her college and withdrew all the money, leaving only Rs 100, as that was the mandatory amount needed at that time to keep the account alive.

Simran knew intuitively that her future and safety lay with Ashok. She desperately tried to contact the officers' ward at the Command Hospital in Pune, but the line was continuously engaged. She didn't have the ALC telephone number. She, however, realized that having run away from home, she needed to have a place to stay until she reached the safety and security that she expected from Ashok. Staying with any of her relatives would be courting disaster, as her father would trace her there. Going to her close college friends would be asking for trouble as well. She, however, remembered Gita, a school friend who lived in a colony called NOIDA that had come up recently on the outskirts of Delhi. After school, Gita and she had attended different colleges but they had kept in touch.

Gita was the daughter of an Army officer, so her father would surely be able to help Simran to contact Ashok. Fortunately, she had Gita's phone number on her so she called her up. Gita's mother answered and informed her that she could find Gita at the British Council Library. Simran felt reassured. Meeting Gita at the library was a far better option than wandering around NOIDA, a place she wasn't familiar with at all. The British Council Library was located at Connaught Place. She hailed an autorickshaw and told the driver where she wanted to go. Fortunately, he knew the place.

Back at Simran's residence, her father was mustering support from all sorts of people to get his daughter back. Through his political contacts, he had sent directions to the police headquarters in Delhi to have Major Ashok Kumar arrested in Pune. He did not realize that neither the police nor the Army authorities would succumb to wild allegations against persons in uniform. While they accepted that no one was above the law, they would not take action on trumped-up charges against Army personnel without reasonable evidence.

The superintendent of police (SP) of Wanowrie Police Station in Pune was sent to interrogate Major Ashok at the ALC. His first challenge was getting past the sentry at the gate.

The SP pompously announced that was there to arrest an Army officer who was at the ALC. 'Sorry, Sahib,' the sentry said, 'you cannot enter without a warrant or at least, a letter of authority.' The SP returned to his police station to inform his superiors, who, in turn, informed Delhi.

The Delhi police escalated the matter and gave directions to the commissioner of police at Pune. The deputy commissioner (DC) was detailed to visit the ALC and given a copy of the telegram from the director general of police, Delhi, explaining the situation and the charges being levelled against Major Ashok.

The DC in Pune called the PA to the Commandant of the ALC and managed to get a positive response to his request for entering the premises. He met the PA and explained to her his reason for being there.

The Commandant was apprised of the situation and he sent for Ashok, who was busy carrying out trials on his artificial leg. Ashok was mystified as to why the Commandant would want to see him. He walked to the Commandant's office in his shorts, as that was the rig worn by amputees when carrying out trials of their artificial legs. The Commandant asked Ashok to sit down, told him that the police wanted to meet him and then asked what he had been up to, to warrant a visit by the police.

Ashok looked quite nonplussed and said, 'Police? Me? I have no idea why the police would want to meet me.' The Commandant then asked for the DC to be sent in.

The DC entered the Commandant's office. He had been trained at the Officers Police Training School at Nasik, and unlike the SP who had come earlier, he understood the protocol and the customs and traditions of the Army. He saluted and introduced himself. 'Good morning, Sir, I am Ajit Pawar, deputy commissioner of police, Pune.' Colonel Thomas, the Commandant, acknowledged his greeting, asked him to sit down and said, 'Yes, Mr Pawar. What can I do for you?'

Pawar handed the Commandant a piece of paper, which turned out to be a telegram. Colonel Thomas put on his reading glasses, read the telegram and introduced Ashok to the DC. Pawar and Major Ashok then shook hands. The Commandant read the contents of the telegram out aloud:

'FIR lodged at New Friends Colony Police Station, New Delhi. FIR alleges that Kumari Simranjeet Singh, daughter of Mr and Mrs P. Singh, residing at New Friends Colony, has been kidnapped by one Major Ashok Kumar who is presently in a military hospital at Pune. Action be initiated to investigate and report back to DG Police Delhi, at the earliest.

Signed
XXXXXXX
IG Police, Delhi

The Commandant asked Ashok whether he knew Kumari Simranjeet Singh.

'Yes, Sir,' he replied, 'she is a close friend.'

'Are you aware of any of the issues mentioned in the telegram?' the Commandant asked.

'No, Sir,' Ashok replied. 'I have no knowledge whatsoever that she is missing, but I do know that her father is forcing her to marry someone against her wishes.'

'Oh!' said the DC, as he registered this bit of information, of which he was not aware.

The Commandant then informed the DC that Major Ashok was the recipient of the Vir Chakra in the recently concluded war with Pakistan, that he had been grievously injured during that conflict resulting in the loss of his leg and that he had been admitted to the ALC for the fitting of an artificial leg. He added that there was no way Major Ashok could have left the premises of the ALC or the Military Hospital without leave, except to go to the city on an 'out pass', and that the movements of all patients were personally supervised by him. Patients could not leave the premises without permission, irrespective of rank, and he, as the Commandant of the ALC, was personally responsible and accountable for all patients entrusted to his charge. He was personally aware that Major Ashok had never left Pune overnight, as he interacted with his patients every day and knew each of them personally.

Pawar appeared to be convinced that Ashok was in no way involved with the incident of Simran's absence from her home. However, he asked Ashok to inform him if and when Simran contacted him.

Ashok reflected on the request for a while and said, 'No. I consider that to be privileged information. Simranjeet is a close friend of mine, and I have no information about how or why she went missing. She is a responsible adult and knows what she is doing. If she contacts me, I will inform the police only if her life is in danger or if she is being threatened in any way. If Simran contacts me, I may share that information with my Commandant, if I consider it necessary, and take his advice. I can, however, assure you that she has not contacted me so far.'

The Commandant and the DC were not only impressed with Ashok's reply, they were also convinced that he was in no way responsible for Simran's absence from her home. The Commandant asked the DC if there was anything more that he wished to ask Major Ashok. Pawar replied, 'No.' The Commandant then told Ashok that he could leave. Pawar continued to sit in the Commandant's office and they discussed the matter further.

Simranjeet smiled as she recollected her conversation with Ashok and what he told her much later about what had happened. Going through the notes in the old hospital files after she had taken over, Simranjeet learnt that the DC Police and the Commandant reached an agreement that should she make an appearance at the hospital, the Army would then inform the police, as it was an issue involving a missing person. The Commandant, however, made a note in the file that the police would take no action without consulting him.

Going back to her memory of her first day away from home, Simran remembered the surprise on Gita's face when she saw her in the library of the British Council. It was only when she was narrating everything to Gita that Simran realized the enormity of the step she had taken and how it would forever change the course of her life. They decided to consult Gita's parents and left for NOIDA. Later that evening, at Gita's house, the family got together to decide on Simran's future course of action. Simran was quite clear that she wanted to be with Ashok. Gita's father offered to buy her ticket to Pune. Fortunately for Simran, Gita and she were of the same height and weight, so Simran could borrow some clothes from her, as she had come with virtually nothing except the clothes that she had on. Gita's father tried to get through to the upper officers' ward of the military hospital, but he too was unsuccessful.

Gita's father bought a ticket on the *Jhelum Express* for Pune, as that was the only train on which a reservation was available. He and Gita dropped her to the station and saw her off. The train was delayed. The *Jhelum Express* was always late!

On arrival at Pune, Simran got a scooter rickshaw and asked the driver to take her to the Command Hospital. He took her to the MI Room of the Command Hospital. From there, she asked for the officers' ward and was told that it was also known as Ward No. 21. The rickshaw driver was told how to get there. Upon arrival at the parking area, she paid the rickshaw driver and walked to the officers' ward.

What she saw amazed her. It was a ward full of young officers. Some were hopping around on one leg, some were trying to race each other on crutches, others were whizzing around on wheelchairs while playing with a ball. There was much shouting and laughter. All were disabled in some way or the other. Many had lost one leg, some had lost both legs, some had lost an arm, one had lost an eye, and some were disfigured and undergoing plastic surgery. The most heartening aspect was that they were all very cheerful. Perhaps it was because they were together, sharing each other's concerns, that helped them face the world together with a brave face. They appeared to be living in the moment and had pushed all thoughts of the future out of their minds.

Simran recalled the lasting impression that these young officers and their positive attitude had made on her, which would remain with her for the rest of her life.

She asked them where Major Ashok was, and a young officer on crutches informed her that this was the lower officers' ward. He said that Major Ashok would be in the upper officers' ward and offered to take her there. The upper officers' ward was at a higher level, which is why the wards were known as the 'upper' and 'lower' officers' wards. They needed to go up a flight of stairs, and the young officer managed to climb the steps very well using his crutches. He told her that he would soon be getting an artificial leg and that he would be re-joining his unit and would be marching, running and climbing again. Simran admired his courage and enthusiasm.

The first flight of steps led to another and these led to the veranda of an imposing barracks. These buildings were built in 1815 and first occupied in 1817 by troops of the East India Company, who had been garrisoned here to fight the armies of the Peshwas during the Anglo–Maratha wars. Built with the grey rocks of the Deccan Plateau, they had stood the test of time and had a strong and stately appearance. Although the buildings' exteriors were old, the insides had been modernized.

They walked across the floor of a wide veranda built of grey granite flagstones. Groups of visitors sat on garden chairs in the veranda talking to the patients, who were as numerous as the officers of the lower officers' ward. Some of the officers could not move around and the visitors had drawn their chairs around their beds. Simran looked for

Ashok in the veranda, but he was not there. He was not inside the ward either. Upon inquiring, she was told that he was in Room No. 10 in the new wing.

They went back into the broad veranda that led to a light-green corridor, which, in turn, led to the veranda of the new wing. They turned left at the end of the corridor. Room No. 10 was the last room. The young officer on crutches was walking slowly and cautiously now, as there was a risk of slipping on the tiled floor. Finally, they reached Room No. 10. The door was open and people were conversing inside. Simran wondered who they were. Her heart was beating fast. This was the moment she had been dreaming about and had long waited for. She knocked on the glass pane of the open door and someone from inside answered, 'Come in.' Ashok was there with two others. They were playing Scrabble on a bed and a nursing sister was watching them.

She entered the room and just stood there. The sister looked at her, then the others.

That moment would remain etched in her memory for all time.

Ashok was speechless when he saw her.

'Simran!' was all he could manage. But that one word meant the entire world to her. The look on his face and that one word included surprise, love, relief and joy. He was as overcome with emotion as she was. She went up to him and gave him a tight hug.

'Have a look at my leg,' he said.

Simran answered, 'We have all the time in the world to look at your leg. I am so grateful to God for keeping you safe.'

'I'm happy you are safe too,' he said.

Simran was puzzled. 'What do you mean?'

'I didn't know where you were or what had happened to you, and there was no way I could leave this place to find out. I called your home and your mother didn't know where you were either. Your father has accused me of kidnapping you, and I have been interrogated by the Pune police.'

The other officers and the sister witnessing this exchange decided to leave Simran and Ashok alone, so they excused themselves and exited the room.

Simran and Ashok had much to catch up on, and they kept filling each other in on everything that had happened until it turned dark. Simran was famished. She had not eaten or drunk anything except for a cup of tea since that morning. Ashok said that while dinner would not be an issue, he was concerned about where she would spend the night.

A nursing orderly entered with Ashok's dinner on a tray and left it on the side table next to his bed.

Ashok had just decided that they would share his dinner when he heard the voices of the nursing sisters in the veranda. The senior sister, the day sister and the night sister were making their evening rounds. This was part of the daily routine when the day sister handed over the care of the patients to the night sister. This was also an opportunity for the senior sister to meet with the patients and discuss any issues they were facing.

It was, however, now well beyond visiting hours and if the sisters found Simran in the room, then they would be duty-bound to ask her to leave. It was therefore essential that the sisters not find out she was there so late in the evening and that too without anyone's permission.

Ashok asked Simran to get into the attached bathroom quickly and close the door. Simran did as she was told. She had just entered the bathroom when the three sisters walked in.

The senior sister noticed that Ashok had not had his dinner as yet. The night sister drew the curtains and fluffed up the pillows. The day sister, who had seen Simran earlier that evening and knew what had happened, looked around the room and was horrified to see Simran's slippers near Ashok's bed. In her flight to the bathroom, Simran had left her slippers behind! Fortunately, the other sisters were on the other side of the bed. The day sister pushed the slippers under the bed with her foot so that the other sisters would not notice. She looked towards the bathroom and noticed that the door was closed. She drew the curtain across the bathroom door to discourage the night sister from checking inside. The senior sister told Ashok to have his dinner before it became cold and asked him if the food was all right and whether he had any problems. Ashok said that all was well and they left. Ashok felt happy and reassured that the day sister had not let him down. Ashok and Simran then shared Ashok's dinner.

Ashok said, 'You better sleep here tonight. You will, however, have to keep going into the bathroom the moment we hear someone from the hospital coming. A nursing orderly should be coming soon in to clear the dishes, and other nursing orderlies will come to make the bed and bring the mosquito net down. You will have to keep out of sight, so you better take a chair into the bathroom and sit there for some time.' Simran did as she was told.

Ashok realized that he would have to seek the co-operation of the day sister and the officers in the rooms in line with his if Simran's presence was to be kept a secret. He walked across and told them what happened, explaining that the hospital authorities discovering Simran in the hospital past visiting hours would make life difficult for both of them. The immediate requirement was to keep her presence hidden. The officers and the day sister looked forward to excitement in the days ahead in an otherwise dull and boring routine.

After the nursing orderlies had finished their routine duties, the officers from rooms 4 to 9 came to meet Simran. They were all happy to join in on the conspiracy. Simran drew the window curtains after they left. Fortunately, each room had its own complement of fresh sheets and pillows in the built-in cupboards, and Simran spent a fairly comfortable night on the couch.

The next morning, the same routine of smuggling Simran into the bathroom whenever the hospital staff made an appearance had to be repeated. A chair had been moved into the bathroom of Room No. 10 so that Simran could sit down during her frequent 'visits' there. That morning, before the morning round, the day sister came to inform Ashok and Simran that the Medical Officer (MO) in charge of the ward would be doing his rounds that morning and that keeping Simran in the bathroom at that time was a risk not worth taking.

The ward MO, a crusty old major, was known to go into great detail. The ward master accompanied him with a notebook, noting down everything that needed to be done and having to answer what had been accomplished and what remained to be done on the next round. The ward MO was particular about cupboards and bathrooms. All of the cupboards and bathrooms were to be left open. He performed a thorough inspection of every room, including the bathrooms.

Simran would obviously need to leave the bathroom when the ward MO arrived. Where could she possibly go?

Visitors were not permitted at that time of the morning, so she could not be seen in the corridors, sitting on the lawn benches, or anywhere else for that matter. Ashok quickly assembled the battle casualties from Rooms 4 to 9, and they came up with a solution, which was: since too many people moved around the ward in the morning, a chair should be placed in Room No. 10's bathroom for Simran to sit in during that time. Just as the ward MO entered Room No. 10, Ashok would cough twice, signalling Simran to move to the bathroom in Room No. 9, the back door of which would be left open. A chair would be placed there as well. All the bathrooms were connected through a corridor at the back of the rooms. After the MO had finished inspecting Room No. 10, Simran would return via the bathroom back door.

That particular morning, for some unknown reason, the ward MO decided to visit the last room first, i.e., Room No. 10, instead of working his way down from Room No. 4 down. The MO entered Room No. 10 with his staff when Simran was already in the bathroom. Ashok coughed twice, allowing Simran to quietly enter the bathroom in Room No. 9.

Simran had no idea that the ward MO was now visiting the wards in reverse order, and that if he went into the bathroom in Room No. 9, he would find her sitting on a chair, and the cat would be out of the bag! Ashok was at a loss for what to do. The day sister was unaware of Simran's whereabouts or the current plan. Ashok indicated to her that he wished to speak with her. She saw that the bathroom door was open and figured out that Simran wasn't there.

Fortunately, the ward MO was busy discussing the bed linen with the senior sister. The day sister went across to Ashok on the other side of the bed, and he whispered to her that Simran was sitting in the bathroom in Room No. 9! The sister immediately realized the implications of this and went across to inform the occupant of Room No. 9 what had happened. The officer in Room No. 9 had also figured it out and had gone to Room No. 8 to discuss what needed to be done.

They decided that Simran should move from bathroom to bathroom until Room No. 4 was inspected by the ward MO and then return to the bathroom in Room No. 10. Simran could have actually moved back to Room No. 10 during the inspection of Room No. 9, but this is what they planned, and it was faithfully followed. The occupant of each room was told that the signal for Simran to move was a cough by the respective occupant and that the officer in Room No. 9 would need to brief Simran about the change in plan and signal her to move to the next bathroom.

After his discussion with the senior sister, the ward MO went to the bathroom in No. 10 and noticed the chair there. 'What is this chair doing in the bathroom?'

he inquired. Ashok had the presence of mind to say that since his leg had been amputated, he needed to sit while having a bath, which was a fact! The ward MO asked the ward master to indent plastic stools for all the bathrooms, so that those who couldn't stand while bathing would have something to sit on. He then moved to Room No. 9. Meanwhile, Simran had moved on to the bathroom in Room No. 8, but Ashok wasn't aware of it and was worried.

Finally, the rounds by the ward MO of the new wing were concluded. He remarked to the senior sister that the officers in the rooms that he had inspected seemed to be having bad coughs and that she should find out what was wrong with them and let him know. The day sister knew why the officers were coughing. She smiled inwardly and assured the senior sister that she would take care of their coughs.

Simran returned to Room No. 10 via the back veranda exhausted, not so much from the physical effort but from the tension. She was, however, smiling.

Meanwhile, in Delhi, Simran's father was not content to leave the search for his daughter to the police. He had not built up his business by relying on others. He trusted no one, was suspicious of everyone and was ruthless in the pursuit of his goals and objectives. He was convinced, quite correctly, that Simran was in Pune and he needed proof from a source other than the police.

There was a Mr Bharadwaj on the staff at his Bombay office who had visited his home in Delhi and had seen Simran, and he would therefore be able to recognize her. He called him up to explain what had happened and asked him to go to the Military Hospital in Pune and trace his daughter. To ensure identification, he faxed a picture of Simran to him.

Mr Bharadwaj duly arrived in Pune the next day and, after making several inquiries, managed to reach the upper officers' ward. He met the duty medical officer and briefed him about the missing girl, explained his mission and showed him Simran's picture. The duty medical officer was unaware of the situation and truthfully declared that he had never seen the girl. Mr Bharadwaj mentioned that the girl's father believed that his daughter was in Pune, that he was in touch with the Army authorities and the police, and that he would be coming shortly to the Military Hospital accompanied by a posse of police to look for his daughter himself. The day sister overheard this conversation. She was also present in the duty room later when there was a call from the registrar of the hospital. Apparently, the Commandant was aware of Simran's father's plans and had said, 'Mr Singh should be allowed to visit the hospital only after obtaining permission from the hospital authorities. However, Major Ashok's rights should not be compromised in any way, and the medical officer in charge of the officers' ward must be present at the meeting between Simran's father and Major Ashok, if a meeting takes place at all.' Having overheard these conversations, the day sister rushed to Ashok's room to pass on all this information before returning to the duty room. She knew both sides of the story by now and was firmly in support of Ashok and Simran.

The situation was escalating and a solution had to be quickly found. The message from the day sister was timely!

Besides the day sister, Simran's presence was also known to the battle casualties in the neighbouring rooms. If interrogated, the sister and the officers would have to speak the truth. A meeting was held in Ashok's room after the senior sister's rounds and after the nursing orderlies had done their duties. One officer was placed outside Room No. 10 to give a warning if anyone else came around.

The consensus of the meeting was that if Simran and Ashok intended to get married, then there was no point in postponing something they were determined to do. They were both adults, and if they got married, then Simran's family would have no claim on their daughter. Besides, the Command Headquarters had issued directives that relatives of battle casualties were to be given priority accommodation in fully furnished rooms close to the hospital and that they would be allowed to stay as long as the battle casualty was under treatment. If Simran and Ashok were to get married, then Simran would have access to this accommodation.

Beyond the lawn of the new wing and the Ashoka trees, a stairway ran along the outside of the boundary wall, leading to the outside world. Officers returning late after using a late night out pass used this unofficial back entrance to the officers' ward. The area was part of the hospital premises and housed the family quarters of the hospital staff so there was no sentry here. It was suggested that Simran use this exit as and when required, to keep herself out of sight of prying eyes until the wedding.

Everyone agreed that this was the best course of action given the circumstances. The date of the arrival of Simran's father was not known, but the wedding needed to take place as quickly as possible. It was also decided that the military and hospital authorities must not be involved in any way, as it would cause embarrassment for all. Two things needed to be organized: arrangements for a marriage ceremony at a mandir nearby and registration at the Registrar of Marriages. As soon as that was done, an application for temporary accommodation for Simran would need to be submitted on a high priority basis.

One of the officers, who used the back staircase every day as part of his early morning walk, mentioned that on his way out, he visited the mandir around 200 metres from the boundary wall of the upper officers' ward. He also knew the pandit of the mandir, so he could fix the ceremony once the date was decided. Another officer who had a scooter offered to make an appointment at the Registrar of Marriages' office. However, an officer was required as a witness at the Registrar's office, so both Ashok and the officer in question would need 'out' passes. No out passes were necessary for those attending the mandir ceremony, as it was within the hospital area itself. A third officer said that he knew an officer in Command Headquarters who could expedite the application for accommodation as an 'emergency case', considering that the officer's wife-to-be was already in station. Since the office of the Registrar of Marriages closed at 5 p.m., the mandir ceremony would have to be held immediately after lunch. The officers concerned set about their tasks, and there was an air of excitement about the whole project, which was now being planned with military precision.

The normal routine of visiting the ALC in the morning for work on their artificial limbs would need to continue.

Everyone, including Ashok, would need to spend some time at the ALC and sign the attendance register to avoid suspicion that something unusual was about to take place.

All the officers of the lower and upper officers' wards had been informed of the wedding, and they were also requested to be part of the *baraat*.[1] They were asked not to discuss it openly and to congregate at the foot of the staircase on the rear boundary wall of the upper officers' ward at 2.30 p.m. They were instructed to arrive in 'twos and threes' in order to avoid drawing attention to themselves. The baraat consisted of thirty-seven officers on crutches and wheelchairs. Simran and Ashok had gone ahead. The pandit was informed not to extend the ceremony beyond thirty minutes, as the couple needed to be at the Registrar's Office on time.

The baraat slowly wound its way towards the mandir because the ground was uneven and there wasn't even a track. Layers of stratified rocks and boulders were strewn on the path, further slowing their movement. This was probably the only baraat in the world composed entirely of disabled persons. The event was no longer a secret, and some nurses and nursing orderlies had gathered at the railings of the boundary wall, viewing this strange procession snaking its way down to goodness knows where. A nursing orderly was dispatched to find out what was going on. He was told truthfully that they were going for a puja at the mandir and that they would be back in thirty minutes.

The pandit at the mandir conducted the marriage with military precision. He had been informed that the parents of both the bride and the groom could not be present due to unforeseen circumstances. The prayers and the *pheras*[2] were completed on time, and Ashok and Simran received his blessings. They were now man and wife.

An autorickshaw was hired and kept waiting outside the mandir for a quick departure. The pandit had stuck to his commitment for a thirty-minute ceremony. The Registrar of Marriages, who had also been told the story and informed about the reason for the urgency, confirmed that he would complete the formalities in a few minutes. He, too, seemed delighted to be part of the conspiracy, which was unfolding like a 'Mills & Boon' story.

By 4.30 p.m., the marriage of Ashok and Simran was registered.

Ashok had requested a 'night out' pass, which had been granted. He and Simran spent their wedding night in a hotel next to Dorabjee's, near Main Street.

Simran's father arrived in Pune the next day, but he was too late—Ashok and Simran were already married. He attempted to prove 'collusion' by the military authorities in his daughter's disappearance, but he couldn't because there was none. Simran's results of the entrance examination for the Armed Forces Medical College had been declared, and she passed with flying colours.

Major General Simran was still walking down memory lane when she noticed that the sky to the east had taken on a rosy hue with the sun about to rise. Nursing orderlies were serving the patients their early morning tea. The kites that had nested in the Ashoka trees for so many years were flying around making their high-pitched cries. Simran remembered these Ashoka trees as mere saplings thirty years earlier. A muezzin was calling his people to prayer, and the distinct strains of the aarti from the Intelligence School mandir heralded the new day.

Simran was relieved that she finally made the time to sit in the veranda and reflect on the events that had changed the course of her life. As she got up to leave, the night sister came up with an envelope marked '*Urgent and Important*'.

The envelope had the crest of the Army Commander Southern Command on it. It was an invitation for her and Ashok to dinner two days later to celebrate their 30th wedding anniversary. The Army Commander had included a small note of apology explaining that the dinner could not be held on the actual day of her anniversary because the Vice Chief of Army Staff, who wished to be present, could not attend due to some important commitments in Delhi.

Simran smiled. The Vice Chief of Army Staff as well as the GOC-in-C Southern Command were both part of that baraat of the thirty-seven young officers from the upper and lower officers' wards at her wedding that had taken place thirty years earlier!

Postscript

Two of the thirty-seven officers who were part of that baraat so many years ago rose to the rank of lieutenant general, two were promoted to the rank of major general, two advanced to the rank of brigadier, one left the Army and joined the Indian Foreign Service, rising to the rank of ambassador, two were killed in anti-terrorism operations and one died in a road accident. Of the remainder, some were invalided out, some were superannuated and some retired in the normal course.

Ashok took early retirement from the Army and went into the corporate world, where he did exceedingly well. Simran and he settled down in Pune and they have two sons: one is a captain in his father's regiment and is married to a captain in the Army Medical Corps. Their other son is working in the corporate sector and is married to a doctor.

The wheel has turned full circle, and perhaps two more stories are in the making as sequels to this story of their parents.

The Last Word

'Life is a great adventure or nothing.'

Helen Keller

Fear is part of our lives, whether one is in the Army or out of it. Field Marshal Sam Manekshaw, one of our most beloved and revered chiefs, once said: 'There is no man who is without fear, and if there is anyone who says that he has not known fear, he is either a liar or a Gorkha.' The Indian Army teaches its soldiers to conquer fear by focusing on the task at hand and moving forward.

At the end of it all, one may ask whether the joy and the sorrow, the laughter and the tears, the partings and the reunions that are part of life in the armed forces, were worth it. The answer in most cases would be an unequivocal 'Yes'. As Abraham Lincoln said: 'And in the end, it's not the years in your life that count; it's the life in your years.' And the comment by that great deaf and blind activist Helen Keller: 'Life is either a great adventure or nothing.'

Life in the armed forces is vibrant and enriching. The values of duty, honour, courage, sacrifice and love come through strongly in these stories. And of these, love is the most important. Love may not be considered a very 'military' word, but it is love for one's country, love for the people of India, love for the men with whom we serve, love for honour and love for the regiment that motivates a soldier to do what he or she does each day, year after year. It is at the altar of this love that armed forces personnel place their lives in the line of fire and, when called upon to do so, make the ultimate sacrifice in battle.

It is tragic that the values uniting the armed forces have little meaning in public life today. While the man in the street holds the armed forces in high esteem, he knows very little about them. These stories, it is hoped, will bring them closer to the men and women in uniform and inspire them to uphold these ideals.

Image source: https://en.wikipedia.org/wiki/Kohima_War_Cemetery

When you go back, tell them of us and say,
For your tomorrow, we gave our today.
(Epitaph to the war dead at the Kohima War Cemetery)

Ian Cardozo
New Delhi, September 2021

Bibliography

Cardozo, Major General Ian, AVSM, SM. *First Five Gorkha Rifles: An Illustrated History*. New Delhi: United Service Institution of India, New Delhi, 2008.

Cardozo, Major General Ian, AVSM, SM. Ed. *The Indian Army: A Brief History*. New Delhi: Centre for Armed Forces Historical Research, United Service Institution of India, New Delhi, 2006.

Chhina, Squadron Leader Rana S. *The Indian Air Force Memorial Book*. New Delhi: IAF Historical Cell, 1996.

Dasgupta, Swapan. Book review of *Adam's Raj Ribs* by Adam Clapham, *Outlook*, 12 February 2007.

History of the Fifth Royal Gurkha Rifles (Frontier Force), Volume II: 1929–1947. UK: Gale & Polden, 1956.

Jagmohan, P.V.S., and Samir Chopra. *The India–Pakistan Air War of 1965*. New Delhi: Manohar Publishers, 2005.

Juneja, V.P. *Indo–Pak War 1971*. New Delhi: New Light Publication, 1971.

Lewin, Ronald. *Slim: The Standard Bearer*. London: Leo Cooper, 1990.

Mason, Philip. *A Matter of Honour*. London: Penguin, 1974.

Nath, Captain Ashok, MA, FRGS. *Izzat: Historical Records and Iconography of Indian Cavalry Regiments 1750–2000*, New Delhi: Centre for Armed Forces Historical Research, United Service Institution of India, 2009.

Palit, Major General D.K., VrC. *Lightning Campaign*. Thomson Press, Delhi, 1972.

Payne, Robert. *The Tortured and the Damned*. Bombay: Inca Publishers, 1977.

Slim, Field Marshal Sir William. *Defeat into Victory*. Cassell & Co., London, 1956.

The Hamoodur Rehman Commission of Enquiry (Pakistan) into the 1971 Indo–Pak War (as declassified by the Government of Pakistan). Lahore: Vanguard, 2001.

Tufail, Air Commodore M. Kaiser. *Great Air Battles of the Pakistan Air Force*. Ferozesons (Pvt.) Ltd, Lahore, 2005.

Notes

1. Captain Courageous

1. A Colonel of the Regiment is not a rank. It is an appointment, i.e., the officer could be a brigadier, a major general, a lieutenant general or a general. He is elected to this appointment by the officers of the regiment. He is required to look at the needs of the regiment and solve issues—informally.

2. A battalion is the basic unit of the infantry and consists of about a thousand men. A brigade normally has three battalions, a division has three brigades and a corps has two/three divisions.

3. A Regimental Medical Officer (RMO) is a qualified medical doctor who is commissioned as an officer in the Army Medical Corps. Each unit has an RMO, whose duty it is to look after the health needs of the unit in peace and war.

4. In recent times, women officers have been admitted into some of the combat arms.

5. Dinner night is a parade. It is a 'sit-down' dinner and is carried out in accordance with the customs of the service and the customs of that particular regiment. The mess silver makes its appearance on the dining table; each piece of silver is a fragment of the regimental history of the unit. The officers have a particular dress code for formal functions in the officers' mess.

6. Mess havildar (sergeant) is a non-commissioned officer who looks at the basic administration of an officers' mess.

2. Jai! Jai Singh!

1. Samurai: a warrior having his roots in the military aristocracy of feudal Japan.

2. In 2015, a referendum was held in the UK to decide which battle had generated the most positive outcome during World War II and the unanimous answer was the Battle of Kohima.

4. It's Never Too Late

1. After a mandatory seven-year period, if a court of inquiry determines that the missing individual is not a prisoner of war or alive in any other capacity, he is declared 'Missing in action—believed killed.'

5. Future Tense

1. Court of inquiry, summary of evidence, court martial: legal procedures appointed by Army authorities to

examine misdemeanours and award punishments if the person concerned is found guilty.

7. The Sign of the Cross

1. Dah: a Naga sword.
2. Basha: a hut made of bamboo or local material with a roof made of straw or other materials.
3. Kote: a secure room where weapons are kept under guard.

8. Matter of Honour

1. The practice of jauhar has been recorded since Muslim invasions during the Middle Ages. Women belonging to the Rajput clan would kill themselves by fire to avoid being raped, becoming slaves or being killed. The vast majority of these jauhar practices were performed in large groups as an act of protest against the invasions and as a way to conserve their cultural pride and honour.
2. In Mumbai, the colours of British Indian regiments can be seen on the walls of the Afghan Church (the Church of St John the Evangelist) and below the choir at St Joseph's R.C. Church, both in Navy Nagar, Colaba.
3. Izzat is an Indian word for honour, reputation and prestige.

9. Regimental Bonds

1. Paltan is how one's battalion is often referred to.

10. Answer to a Prayer

1. Sorpotel with sannas is a traditional Goan meal of pork curry with steamed rice cakes.

11. Destiny

1. Indochina (originally Indo–China) is a geographical term originating in the early nineteenth century for the continental portion of the region now known as Southeast Asia. It corresponds to the present-day areas of Myanmar, Thailand, Laos, Cambodia, Vietnam and (variably) peninsular Malaysia.
2. The order of battle (ORBAT) gives the composition of a force by number, nomenclature and type.
3. Camping in the open using improvised methods to provide shelter from the elements of nature.
4. The Admin Box is a short form for Administrative Box. In order to fight and not withdraw, formations had been ordered by Slim to be self-contained as far as possible. The administrative elements in this instance were grouped together just behind the fighting elements to carry out their administrative functions, and this was labelled as the Admin Box.

12. The Memento

1. Fauji: a soldier.

13. Ward No. 21

1. Baraat: An Urdu word that describes the groom's wedding procession in north and west India, where it is

customary for the groom to travel to the wedding venue accompanied by his family members and friends.

2. This is one of the most important rituals of a Hindu wedding. *Saat-Phere* requires the bride and groom to go around the sacred fire seven times, reciting specific Vedic mantras, and keeping the holy fire as witness to the vows they make to one another on each circuit.